THEY WALKED A CROOKED MILE

Picture Research   MARION GEISINGER

HART PUBLISHING COMPANY, INC., New York City

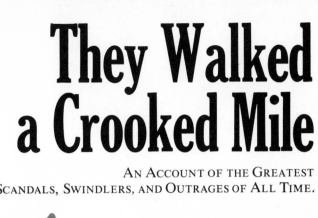

They Walked
a Crooked Mile

An Account of the Greatest
Scandals, Swindlers, and Outrages of All Time.

CHARLES FRANKLIN

CONTENTS

LIST OF ILLUSTRATIONS

THE GREAT SOUTH SEA BUBBLE

THE DREYFUS AFFAIR

TEAPOT DOME

THE SWINDLES OF CLARENCE HATRY

THE ENGLISH PENAL COLONIES

HARRY THAW: MURDERER

CHILD LABOR

HENRY VIII AND HIS SIX WIVES

THE FRENCH GALLEY SLAVES

VAN MEEGEREN: MASTER FORGER

ACKNOWLEDGMENTS

AUTHENTICATED NEWS INTERNATIONAL, 170 Fifth Avenue, New York
86, 337 *(bottom)*, 339

THE BETTMANN ARCHIVE, 136 East 57th Street, New York
117, 118, 119, 323, 330-331, 370-371, 379, 384-385

BROWN BROTHERS, 220 West 42nd Street, New York
221, 225, 228-229, 233, 234, 273, 275, 277, 278, 285, 286, 288, 290, 293, 296

CULVER PICTURES, INC., 660 First Avenue, New York
107, 198-199, 205 *(top)*, 359

HISTORICAL PICTURES SERVICE, 2753 West North Avenue, Chicago
57, 58-59, 62-63, 65, 66, 74, 78-79 *(2)*, 80, 81, 82-83, 84, 316, 325, 327, 333 *(2)*, 334, *(2)*, 335 *(top)*, 336
(2), 337 *(top)*

KEYSTONE PRESS AGENCY, 170 Fifth Avenue, New York
250

LORD CHAMBERLAIN, St. James's Palace, London SW1
177, 182-183

THE MANSELL COLLECTION, 42 Linden Gardens, London W2
69, 114, 264-265, 266, 312, 313, 314-315, 318-319, 372-373 *(2)*, 375 *(2)*, 376-377

NATIONAL PORTRAIT GALLERY, Trafalgar Square, London SW1
172, 347

17

PICTORIAL PARADE, 130 West 42nd Street, New York
124, 125, 132, 134, 136, 139, 141, 149, 151, 154, 159, 162, 164,
165

PIX, INC., 236 East 42nd Street, New York
131, 150, 160

PAUL POPPER, LTD., 24 Bride Land, Fleet Street, London EC4
127, 143, 144, 146, 244, 253, 392-393

PROFESSIONAL PICTURE SERVICE, 147 West 42nd Street, New York
51, 52-53, 61, 70, 72-73, 93, 96-97, 99, 101, 102, 170-171, 178-
179 *(2)*, 180-181, 186, 190-191, 193, 195, 196-197, 200, 202-203,
204, 205 *(bottom)*, 206 *(2)*, 208-209, 210, 211, 212, 213, 214, 216,
227, 329, 335 *(bottom)*, 343, 344, 349, 350, 353, 354, 361, 362, 381

RADIO TIMES HULTON PICTURE LIBRARY, 35 Marylebone High Street,
London W1
258, 261, 262, 269, 311, 368-369, 380, 382-383

UNITED PRESS INTERNATIONAL, 220 East 42nd Street, New York
24, 28, 32-33, 34-35, 37, 38, 40-41, 43, 112, 128, 152-153, 156,
163, 222, 231, 236-237, 238, 247, 249, 252, 255, 280-281, 289,
295, 298, 299, 302-303 *(2)*, 304, 305, 306, 396-397

WIDE WORLD PHOTOS, INC., 50 Rockefeller Plaza, New York
88-89

PREFACE

Why a compendium of swindles and outrages? Because the ever developing history of mankind requires the casting of a rapid eye over its follies as well as its glories.

Here, then, is a rogue's gallery of the arch perpetrators of con games, sadistic cruelties, and religious immoralities—callous crooks, sanctimonius hypocrites, unspeakable blackguards, meglomaniac finaglers, and heartless tyrants who have marched through the pages of history.

Some of these glimpses will horrify you; some may amuse you. All are likely to fascinate.

THEY WALKED A CROOKED MILE

CHARLES PONZI: SUPER-CHARLATAN

Confidence men rely on the greed and credulity of their victims. As P. T. Barnum said, "There's a sucker born every minute," ready to believe any plausible rogue.

Charles A. Ponzi, a diminutive, picturesque, Italian immigrant was a slick operator into whose hands 40,000 Bostonians pressed $15,000,000 during the year 1920. In one single day, a horde of the gullible, seeking easy lucre, showered the swindler with two million in cold cash, obtaining no security other than Mr. Ponzi's personal note. For Ponzi had promised his investors a return of 50% interest in 90 days; and to those sufficiently patient to wait six months, the deal was double your money back.

It was an irresistible ploy. Ponzi explained that he had a simple scheme. World War I had left the monetary systems of Europe in chaos; all European currencies had severely depreciated vis a vis the American dollar. Ponzi had agents throughout Europe who were engaged in buying depreciated European specie with his investors' money. With this currency, Ponzi's agents bought international postal reply coupons. When these international postal coupons were transferred to the United States they could be redeemed, so Ponzi alleged, at their face value for American dollars. Thus a postal coupon bought in Europe with European money equivalent to 50¢ in American money, could be transmuted in the United States into a full American dollar. The announcement of this alchemy brought

CHARLES PONZI   *On August 2, 1920, in the midst of a panic and investigations and newspaper attacks, the jaunty financier still appears confident.*

thousands of people to Ponzi's doors clamoring for him to accept their money and make them rich overnight.

Who was the financial wizard who had figured out this ingenious plan? Charles A. Ponzi, born in Parma, Italy in 1882, had emigrated to America when he was 17, landing in Boston with "$2.50 in cash and a million dollars in hopes." He asserted that he was the scion of a well-to-do Italian family, and had studied at the University of Rome where he had been something of a spendthrift. He felt, he said, that he had to get down to honest work, so he had cut himself off ruthlessly from his wealthy connections in Italy and had come to America to seek his fortune. That, at least, was his story.

Here, in the golden land, he had worked at various jobs. He had been a waiter and a dishwasher in New York, then a sign painter in Florida. In 1917, he had returned to Boston to take a job with a brokerage firm at $25.00 a week. A year later, he married Rose Guecco, the daughter of a fruit vendor. And by 1919, Charles A. Ponzi was in the big money.

A boom had started which was to last through the 20's. Wages were high, and there was an unprecedented demand for luxuries. Automobiles were rapidly becoming a necessity; the womenfolk of the laboring classes were clamoring for better clothes, more frequent visits to the movies, and higher education for their children. To provide all these needs, increased income was needed, and Ponzi held out this hope.

Ponzi's Securities Exchange Company occupied dingy offices at 27 School Street, Boston, with an entrance in Pie Alley. Inside these offices, there were no furnishings; the only decor was a mass of greenbacks overflowing from battered desks onto the floor—and that was all that was needed. For months, the place was under constant siege by investors. For the wonder worker paid 50% profit within 45 days on every dollar deposited with him. His clients were hysterically enthusiastic.

Every day, the dapper homonculus—he was no more than

five feet two inches tall—arrived at his office in his splendid blue limousine. He was immaculate, straw-hatted, always wore a fresh flower in his buttonhole, and in dashing continental style, held a cane over his arm.

Every day, as he arrived at his office, Charles A. Ponzi was greeted by an ecstatic mob who waved their folding money at him, eagerly thrusting their savings into his hands. To get a share of the action, some people sold their Liberty bonds; others, who had no savings, borrowed from loan sharks to invest with Ponzi. Some of his heaviest investors were police officials. And the take was so brisk and of such dimension that the steady withdrawal of funds from savings accounts began to cause concern in banking circles.

The more sophisticated citizenry, of course, were not duped; the skeptical sensed that there must somewhere be a catch in all this. But the small people, the working people, the people who had never had any hand in financial transactions were only too willing to believe that a magician had dropped into their midst and would make them rich overnight. Hadn't he already done so for Frank the butcher, and John the baker, and Izzy the tailor, and Enrico the shoemaker. In particular, his fellow Italians lionized him.

If anyone evinced suspicion of the financier, indicating that Ponzi might be swindling his investors, a fellow Italian would say, "He would never dare to treat his own people like that. They would cut his heart out with a knife."

Pretty soon, the traffic at Pie Alley was so great that Ponzi came into national prominence. In July, 1920, the federal authorities began an investigation of his activities. The postal people were able to prove that Ponzi had not made the enormous profits he claimed by buying international reply coupons, asserting that the entire amount redeemed by the United States during the preceding 12 months would be insufficient to account for even a small fraction of the money that Ponzi claimed that he had made through this kind of manipulation. The French Ministry of Finance chimed in with the statement that Ponzi's claims were utterly specious, and that he would have had to pay a full American dollar for a dollar's worth of coupons, that his story of his fabulous exchange manipulations was indeed nothing more than a fable.

In Boston, the *News Bureau,* a daily financial paper published by C. W. Barron, financial expert, ridiculed the whole scheme in such violent terms that Ponzi immediately filed a $5,000,000 libel suit against the publisher.

Interviewed by the *New York Evening World,* Ponzi said:

> *You know, this whole fracas at present is due to just one state of affairs. Bankers and businessmen can easily understand how I could make 100% for myself, but simply because no one has ever made an added 50% for the general public, they reason it can't be. The truth is bankers and businessmen have been doing plenty for themselves under the present banking system, but they have done little for anybody else.*
>
> *I want to change this unfair condition. The depositor in the banks today is not getting a square deal. I shall endeavor to create an institution where the depositor will get what he ought to get, even if it does shake up the old crowd. Now please do not think I am boasting, but I have forgotten more about foreign exchange than C. W. Barron ever knew.*
>
> *Yes, I know it is a shock to some of these folks who have been hogging it all, but it is fair and right, and the depositor should get a fair return for his money.*

For all his big talk, informed people and solid bankers rea-

soned that Ponzi's rapid acquisition of wealth was achieved by robbing Peter to pay Paul, and that Charles A. was simply using the money he accepted from one batch of investors to pay his debts to an earlier batch of investors. But, at the moment, no one could prove that this was the case.

Meanwhile, the diminutive Ponzi increased his stature, rhetorically speaking, in the business world. He bought a large interest in the Hanover Trust Company, and became a director of that bank. He bought J. B. Poole Company, importers and exporters, outright—the place he had once worked at, as a stock boy. By the end of July, 1920, it was estimated that Ponzi had a capital of $8,000,000.

But on July 26, 1920, Boston District Attorney Pelletiere ordered Ponzi to cease accepting any more investments until an official auditor had examined his accounts to determine whether his company could meet all its outstanding obligations and was "functioning in a safe and legitimate manner." Ponzi raised no objection. In fact, he said that in view of what was being maliciously said about him, he would welcome the scrutiny. He alleged that his outstanding indebtedness totaled $3,000,000, and that he had several million dollars more than that sum on deposit in banks in both Boston and in Europe to cover those liabilities.

But when it got about that United States Government auditors had also descended on Ponzi, the news touched off something of a panic, and Pie Alley was besieged. The long line of withdrawers received both their principal and their interest in full, and everyone waiting in line was supplied—at Ponzi's expense—with coffee, hot dogs, and sandwiches. It now appeared that the full panoply of investigation had fallen upon Ponzi's operations. The Attorney General of Massachusetts, the District Attorney of Boston, and the Assistant U. S. Attorney of the federal government were all examining Ponzi's books and accounts. On the face of it, there was nothing irregular in Ponzi's business. All entries of intake from and payments to investors had been properly kept, and yet everyone involved in the investigations sensed that Ponzi's operation was a swindle. For Ponzi refused to divulge the source of his profits, and defied the government to learn the secrets of his operations, saying:

> *I am in business to make money. Ethics do not interest me any more than it interests banks. These coupons are used as currency in Europe. My secret is*

how I cash the coupons. I do not tell it to anybody.
Let the United States find it out if it can.

Meanwhile Ponzi was obliged to pay out vast sums to those who had lost faith in him. On Thursday, July 29, cash from the bank was brought to the Ponzi offices by armed guards, and cash was paid out to anyone who stood in line and presented a Ponzi receipt. There was so much cash in Ponzi's office that his teller was flanked by a young man who held a revolver. At the close of that day, Miss Lucy Meli, Ponzi's young and pretty secretary, announced that nearly $2,000,000 had been paid out to the public since the previous Monday. She added that Ponzi was handling some 50,000 accounts representing investments ranging from $10 to $40,000, the average investment around $3,000.

Despite this display of good faith, Ponzi was not permitted to receive any more funds from the public. Nevertheless, at the very time that he was being scrutinized under the microscope by every investigative power, workers in factories and in department stores were forming pools and were impatiently waiting to be allowed to hand their money over for the promise of a 50% yield in 45 days.

On July 31, U. S. Attorney Gallagher announced that he soon hoped to establish the facts beyond question, and that announcement seemed ominous enough to many. On August 2, Ponzi's former publicity agent, one McMasters, alleged that Ponzi had never issued or received a foreign draft. In consequence, another panic broke out, but despite the big run on his funds, Ponzi was able to honor every bit of paper presented by worried claimants.

The situation was strangely ambiguous: scores of people were running pell mell to Ponzi to get their money back, and other scores of people were still willing to give Ponzi—despite the hue and the cry—the very shirts off their backs.

The run on Pie Alley continued on August 3. Huge funds were disbursed by the smiling Ponzi who said, "Mountains of money are available to pay all claims. All the boys and girls have to do is to drop in and get it." From what inexhaustible cache was all this specie coming?

The official United States auditor, Edwin Pride, still working on the Ponzi books, was astounded at the torrent of money that Ponzi was disbursing, and admitted to the press that he had never seen so much ready cash in all his life. The beaming Ponzi returned the compliment by offering Mr. Pride a job as head bookkeeper in the new hundred million dollar investment syndicate he was planning.

But the following day, the smile on Ponzi's face faded away when J. Weston Allen, the Massachusetts Attorney General, suggested putting an auditor to work on Ponzi's accounts to find out *the exact amount of Ponzi's assets.* Ponzi bluntly refused, maintaining there was no law that could force him to show how much he was worth. He maintained that Pride was investigating the extent of his liabilities, and that when the full amount of his debts was established, he—Ponzi—would produce enough cash to cover all claims.

That same night, Ponzi took his young wife to the theater, where their appearance in a box was greeted with loud cheers. The dapper little man personified success; in reality, he was on the verge of ruin.

The blow fell on August 9, when Bank Commissioner Joseph C. Allen declared Ponzi's account overdrawn and directed the Hanover Trust Company to cease honoring Ponzi's checks. Ponzi claimed that he had a credit of a million and a half dollars at the Hanover Trust Company. The Attorney General held that Ponzi's balance was a mere $121,436.

Official investigators, disinterring every clue that Ponzi's books could yield, found nothing at all to confirm the allegation that his dealings in international coupons had been on a million dollar scale. The authorities now bluntly asserted that the swindler never had received any funds at all from Europe worth talking about.

"In view of the facts disclosed," said the Attorney General, "I invited Ponzi to come and explain. He has failed to take advantage of the opportunity."

A more telling blow was dealt with the revelation on August 11 that Ponzi had served a three-year sentence in Canada for forgery, and later had spent three years in an Atlanta jail for violating United States immigration laws by smuggling three Italians across the Canadian border. Now Ponzi no longer smiled; he wept as he admitted his past, and was furious at the way "the authorities were persecuting him." Interestingly, the disclosures failed to shake the confidence of many of his investors, who still believed that his postal coupon gimmick was on the level regardless of what the great manipulator might have done in the past.

Ponzi now recognized that his end was at hand. He knew that if his credulous investors learned the truth, they would turn on him with all the fury of the betrayed. He immediately

EVIDENCE   Certificates such as this one led to Ponzi's downfall.

October 24ᵈ 192

Certificate No.   1

Name Rose M. Ponzi

187 Strathmore rd.

35 Brighton, Mass
     Units of Indebted

$350ᵒᵒ

Redeemable at $1,050 ᵒᵒ

installed armed guards at his Lexington mansion, and always carried a loaded pistol in his pocket. Two days later, he was arrested on two warrants: one charged him with using the United States mails with intent to defraud; the other charged him with larceny by false pretenses.

Now there were wild scenes outside his closed offices. His enraged victims howled for their money. Some of his agents and assistants were arrested. And so, too, were the operators of a rival concern, the Old Colony Foreign Exchange Company, which had been imitating Ponzi's methods on a lesser scale.

Terrified that he would be lynched by those he had duped, Ponzi sought the safety of jail. The police preferred him there, too, in order to insure whatever assets he had would be preserved for his creditors, and not secreted by him for future use. Bail, it was rumored, would be set at a prohibitively high figure. The authorities believed that Ponzi had salted away huge sums by making deposits in the names of others. If his wife was holding concealed assets, such funds would be confiscated.

However, on that unlucky Friday, the 13th of August, Mrs. Ponzi was actually unaware that her husband had been taken

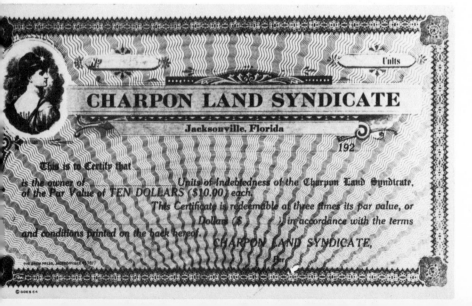

WORRIED INVESTORS Nervous crowds keep a watchful eye on the Hanover Trust Company where Ponzi had deposited much of their money.

to prison. Apologizing for his absence, she smilingly entertained friends in their Lexington mansion, all of whom knew what had happened, though none had the heart to tell her. Meanwhile, from the East Cambridge jail where he was being held, Ponzi phoned the guards surrounding his house not to allow any newspaper men to enter the grounds, and to keep all

newspapers from being delivered to their home so that his wife wouldn't learn about the debacle. But the following day, Rose Ponzi found out what had happened, and she obtained permission to visit her husband in jail. Still full of confidence, Ponzi reassured her that he would be back in business within a couple of weeks. Now, day by day, in her blue limousine and accompanied by two guards, Rose Ponzi trekked back and forth between her splendid Lexington home and her husband's dingy cell, bringing Charles supplies of fresh linen and cigarettes. A battery of attorneys was busy preparing his defense.

A report gained currency that the swindler was going to plead "financial dementia." If nothing else, this defense was certainly novel; it was to be built on statements by those who had known the man for years, and who would maintain that Ponzi had always been working on hare-brained schemes for amassing riches.

On August 20, Ponzi admitted he was unable to pay his liabilities and was taken before Referee Olmstead in the United States Bankruptcy Court. To the shock of 10,550 creditors, whose claims amounted to $4,308,874.73, on August 24 that court declared Ponzi a bankrupt. The prisoner gave evidence of assets deposited in numerous banks, and disclosed loans made to various companies and individuals for which he held notes. When Ponzi was asked whether he had sent money abroad, he replied: "No money for business purposes. I decline to answer any more questions of this kind on the ground that it might incriminate me." After he had taken refuge behind the Fifth Amendment, there was little or nothing more that his further examination could reveal.

But Lucy Meli, his young confidential secretary, was called to the stand. Upon examination, she declared that she knew only about office transactions and nothing about Ponzi's business done on the outside.

"Were there any international reply coupons in your office?" Attorney Dodge inquired.

"Yes, one or two as samples," the girl innocently answered. Ponzi, who was sitting near the rail talking to his wife, looked up and laughed outright.

The attorney continued: "Was any money sent abroad to purchase international coupons?"

SPRUNG Temporarily free on $14,000 bail, Charles Ponzi is shown in 1924, between the two jail sentences he served for different counts of fraud. Woman at far left is unidentified; the two others are Mrs. Rose Ponzi and Mrs. C. Malaguiti.

Yes, replied Lucy, some money had been sent abroad, but she did not know for what purpose. Enough was sent, she added, to purchase about 100,000 lira. The amount was ludicrous.

Two days later, the court's receivers descended upon Ponzi's Lexington estate and seized the house, the furniture, and his three motor cars. Rose Ponzi was in tears. All her fair weather friends had deserted her.

"I have dismissed all my servants," she informed the *New York Times*. "I have today sent my automobile to town to the authorities, and they will probably sell it to someone for a couple of thousand dollars. They can add that to the assets. I am penniless and without friends, but thank God, I am strong and can work."

She then went to visit her husband in jail, riding in a street car. She was permitted to remain in the Lexington mansion

PONZI'S HOME   When Ponzi went bankrupt, authorities seized his $100,000 mansion in Lexington, Massachusetts, along with his furniture, cars, and his other assets. Mrs. Rose Ponzi was temporarily permitted to stay in the house, until she could locate a "small tenement" to serve as her new home.

while she looked for a "small tenement" in which to live. She had been a bookkeeper before her marriage, and soon had offers of several positions.

According to Pride's final figures, Ponzi had accepted $9,814,884.70 from the public and had paid back $7,824,-650.77. He had swindled about $2,000,000, much of which the court's receivers were able to recover. Later figures estimated Ponzi's take to be as much as 15 million.

When on October 21, the Federal Grand Jury in Boston indicted him on 43 counts, Ponzi claimed he was penniless—he was in fact, so indigent he didn't even have enough money to pay for counsel. He defended himself at his trial, was found guilty and was sentenced to five years imprisonment in the federal jail at Plymouth.

How can one explain Charles A. Ponzi? The best guess is that he was a poor immigrant who compensated for his early poverty with delusions of grandeur. The little man yearned to be big and powerful.

Perhaps, one day, his grandiose talk of being able to manipulate funds and turn huge profits was challenged by some friend or fellow worker who put $10 into his hands and dared him carry out his boast and double the sum. Perhaps, not wishing to appear to be a blowhard, Ponzi had repaid that $10 with $20, whereupon the recipient spread the news far and wide. Probably, then, others who had heard of the exploit beat a path to Ponzi's door and offered the miracle maker more money. And Ponzi couldn't refuse. For one thing, he would lose face; and for another, he simply basked in the admiration bestowed upon him, and reveled in the trust and confidence he had created.

Once in, he had to keep up the show and return huge interest on every dollar he received. He was able to do this because money from still other people poured so fast into his coffers. Drunk with success, the little man put off all reckoning. Per-

PANIC   At Ponzi's bank in Boston, disillusioned investors clamor for their money.

haps he himself believed that somehow with all that cash on hand he would be able to make some sound investments here and there—perhaps a killing now and then—that would permit him to fulfill his extravagant promises. Undoubtedly, his megalomania blinded him to the fact that he was inevitably headed toward disaster.

After his release from prison in 1924, he was re-arrested and tried again on some of the remaining charges. In July, 1925, Judge Sisk in Boston sentenced him to state's prison for a further term of seven to nine years, adjudging him a "common and notorious thief." When in 1934, Ponzi was finally released, having served the full nine years, he was deported to Italy.

There he obtained a job with an Italian airline and was sent to Rio de Janeiro. When that airline folded, Ponzi was once again penniless, and he ended up in a charity ward, half blind and partly paralyzed. He died in Brazil in 1949 at the age of 66.

At the height of his success, Charles A. Ponzi was hailed by those he was cheating as the greatest Italian who ever lived. "You're wrong," he modestly told them, "there's Columbus who discovered America, and Marconi who discovered the wireless."

"But you discovered money," they told him.

DEPORTED   On October 7, 1934, immigration officers escort Charles Ponzi aboard the "Vulcania."

SCANDALS OF THE MEDIEVAL CHURCH

During medieval times, the corruptions of the Church of Rome ran the gamut of every evil to which man falls prey. Scandals and abuses riddled the hierarchy from the Papal throne right down to the parish priest. Sexual lapses were rife among the clergy; perversion and bestiality plagued monastery and convent.

The early Christian church had declared sex to be a vile sin. Tertullian, an influential early churchman of the second century, had proclaimed that sex was the "essence of sin," and that woman was the "gate of hell." Ambrose (c. 340-397) taught that chastity was more important than basic doctrine. This saint sincerely believed that even the extinction of the human race was preferable to its propagation by sin. Consequently, among very early Christians, especially would-be saints, self-castration had been a frequent gesture. The most notable example of this cast of thought was the third century teacher Origen (c. 185-251), who hoped to gain heaven by turning himself into a eunuch. One Anglo-Saxon queen was actually canonized for refusing to have intercourse with her husband.

From Paul on, the tradition was stern and unremitting. Sex, as such, was to be avoided as the most heinous of sins; it was to be indulged in only to beget children.

But, of course, as the Bible itself points out, love is stronger than the grave, and the call of the flesh could not be denied, even among those who were pledged to everlasting celibacy and chastity. Needless to say, churchmen were not the only transgressors. But since the Church condemned concupiscence so roundly and so unremittingly, the gulf between the pretention and the practice of the clergy was utterly shocking to the truly devout who accepted all scriptural and ecclesiastical pronouncements at face value.

In medieval days, the nobility, both secular and clerical, enjoyed almost unlimited privilege. Practically immune to prosecution under laws which they themselves made and controlled, the ruling classes could pursue their inclinations with great latitude—and they did.

Many churchmen, more self-controlled, attempted to regulate and reform their fellows. Several sets of rules were put into effect, prescribing exact penances for sexual abberrations. The English theologian Bede (672-735), produced the most detailed of the Anglo-Saxon penitentials. According to his fiat, adultery was punishable with a sentence of fasting from two to seven years.

St. Ecgbert, archbishop of York during the eighth century, ordained special penances for unusual postures of love-making between husband and wife. His list of transgressions also covered every imaginable combination of a human consorting with an animal. Under Sir Ecgbert's code of 729, a monk who fornicated with a woman was required to fast for three years; and his female partner, for two years. If a layman seduced a nun, he would incur a two-year penalty of fasting, and she would suffer the same consequence for three years. But if a child was born, the deprivation would extend to four years; and if they slew the child, retribution extended to seven years.

St. Ecgbert also ordained that a habitually homosexual bishop would have to do similar penance for 14 years; and that a bishop who fornicated with cattle should be punished by an eight-year fast for a first offense, and by a ten-year fast for repeated malfeasance. The Saint's eye pried into every corner of the realm of sex. He decreed that if a man copulated with his wife "like a dog," he should be made to fast for seven years; and that if he enjoyed conjugal relations on a Sunday, he could expiate the sin only by three days' full penance. And so on and so on.

Some three hundred years later, the code of King Canute (1015-1035) was even more strict, and provided that an adulterer would be deprived—not only of his right to marry again—but also of his nose and his ears.

Similar codes existed through the centuries. Nevertheless, offenders among the clergy often went unscathed—first because such men were part of the very establishment which administered the laws, and secondly because the Church could not afford to lose the services of every capable man who was guilty of sexual misdeeds. An offender, though sometimes deposed from his exalted station, was more often merely transferred to an equally lucrative benefice.

In the late medieval period, lapses from clerical celibacy were never universally prosecuted. However, sporadic attempts were made to enforce priestly continence; and at times, offenders were savagely chastised. In the 11th century, Pope Gregory VII, who ruled from 1073 to 1085, instituted several reforms. During his reign, a number of priests who had married were caught up by the mob and castrated and then exposed in their mutilated state to the public. Gregory's successor, Urban II, simply offered the wives of priests as slaves to any nobleman who would accept them.

In 1126, Cardinal Giovanni of Cremona was sent by Pope Honorius II to restore discipline among the English clergy. He called a meeting of the Synod of London, and denounced concubinage among British priests. That very night, however, he himself was surprised in bed with a prostitute. He may very likely have been framed by the hostile English clergy. At this late date, proof is unavailable.

The Council of Constance (1414-1418), called to institute church reform, must have been quite a lively gathering. Lasting four years, it was attended, according to the contemporary chronicler Gebhard Dacher, by 18,000 priests, 83 wine merchants, 346 "clowns, dancers, and jugglers," and 700 undisguised whores. These were the 700 prostitutes whose addresses Dacher was able to obtain. A list drawn up in Vienna lists 1,500 "common harlots" (*meretrices vagabundae*) present at the Council. It is likely that thousands of other camp followers attended this great Church conclave but remained unidentified either by Dacher or by the Viennese chronicler. It is recorded that at least one lady attended the Council and was able to retire for life, having earned through her favors to the clergy, some 800 florins, a sizable sum in those days.

One of the most sincere and impassioned reformers of the late melieval period was Girolamo Savonarola who was born of a poor family in Ferrara, Italy, in 1452, and who turned to the monastic life. Donning the habit of the Dominicans, the "Order of Preachers," in 1474, he was sent eight years later to Florence, the capital of the Italian Renaissance and seat of the immensely powerful Medicis, the banking family. From his pulpit at San Marco, Savonarola inveighed not only against the immoralities that the Florentine clergy took for granted, but against the paganization of the city's churches as well. In a Florence where degenerate young men with painted lips and penciled eyebrows lingered decoratively on the steps and among the columns of the most famous churches, and where statues of Venus were carried in religious processions beside those of the Virgin Mary, Savonarola denounced the wantonness of the Church. "Oh, prostitute Church," he thundered. "You have become a shameful harlot in your lusts! You have displayed your foulness to the whole world, and you stink to high heaven!"

Savonarola's popularity as a preacher in licentious Florence spread slowly at first, but gathered strength as his conviction grew that he was a divinely inspired prophet. He believed it his mission to cleanse the city of the moral filth and blatant paganism sponsored by the most illustrious of the Medicis, Lorenzo the Magnificent. Despite Lorenzo's disfavor and the bitter enmity of Pope Alexander VI, Savonarola's fiery sermons attracted such masses of Florentines that the churches could not contain them and he took to preaching out of doors.

In 1494, when the Medici were temporarily overthrown by a popular revolution, Savonarola became virtual dictator of the city. Prostitutes, formerly so bold that even monks were accosted and matrons openly insulted on the streets, disappeared. The city's notorious traffic in obscene pictures was halted. Books, paintings, and other vehicles of pagan influence were burned; even carnival seasons were turned into times of public penance and mass contrition.

But the deprivations imposed upon them were too arduous for the Florentines. In 1498, they turned against their once-beloved preacher. In April of that year he was arrested and subjected to merciless and prolonged tortures which wrenched his limbs from their sockets. On May 23, he was hanged and burned as a heretic.

Despite sporadic reformers such as Savonarola, the medieval world and its prelates remained corrupt. Pope John XII, who ruled from 955 to 964, kept a harem in the Lateran Palace. This man, who became Pope at the age of 18 through the influence of his family, was later deposed on grounds of perjury, murder, sacrilege, and incest. Nearly 500 years later, Pope John XXIII (later declared an anti-Pope) lived a similarly profligate life. This John XXIII, who reportedly had poisoned his predecessor and purchased his office, was deposed by the Council of Constance in 1415 on formal grounds

GIROLAMO SAVONAROLA   *Educated by his grandfather, a doctor steeped in medieval scholasticism, Savonarola, at age twenty-two turned from his medical studies to enter the Dominican order at Bologna. As a teacher and lecturer, he soon became famous for his learning and for his asceticism.*

In the Lenten seasons of 1485 and 1486, he began preaching his famous prophetic sermons. He alleged that the church needed reforming, but that to be reformed, she must first be scourged, and only then renewed. As he warmed to his theme, his sermons became increasingly bold; and in 1490, he was preaching openly against the abuses in government. When the Medici family fell from power, Savonarola was left in effective control of the city of Florence. Virtual dictator of the city, he imposed stringent measures to encourage asceticism. Under his influence, the 1497 carnival, departing from its usual pattern of revels and debauches, was devoted to repentance. The formerly wild and gay carnival now featured sacrificial bonfires of personal ornaments, lewd paintings, cards, gaming tables, and other worldly items.

Savonarola's restrictions, however, were too much for many people—including His Holiness. Pope Alexander VI, a worldly man, first invited and then ordered Savonarola to report to him for correction. Savonarola replied to the Pope's summons of 1495 by pointing out eighteen errors in His Holiness's letter, adding for good measure, a few trenchant comments about the Pope's personal life.

Finally, all the anti-Savonarola interests united and won the support of the rabble. In 1498, Savonarola was seized and tortured. But even after subjecting him to prolonged torment, his detractors were obliged to falsify the records to fabricate charges against him that would stand up. His death was in the best tradition of martyrdom: before mounting the scaffold, Savonarola received the Pope's absolution which forgave all his sins and gave him instant entry to Heaven. After he was hanged, his body was burned.

Many Catholics—even some who themselves were later canonized by the church—have venerated Savonarola as a saint. In 1952, the 500th anniversary of his birth, there was again widespread talk of canonizing the reformer of Florence.

HIERONYMI·FERRARIENSIS·A·DEO·
MISSI·PROPHETÆ·EFFIGIES·

SAVONAROLA'S BONFIRE   *In the famous "bonfire of vanities," citizens of Florence destroy their books, their paintings, and their other "pagan" possessions.*

Although at this time they followed Savonarola's preaching and burned their worldly goods, later they changed their minds—and burned Savonarola.

of "notorious heresy, complacency in schism, simony, dilapidation of church properties, misconduct, and incorrigibility." The detailed charges against him included homicide, atheism, incest, adultery, and dozens of other counts—most of them well substantiated.

Many archbishops and abbots installed, not only hawks and hounds, but women—either in abbeys or other residences. Illegitimate children were legion. In 1171, one Clarembald, abbot-elect of St. Augustine's foundation at Canterbury, boasted that he had fathered 17 bastards in one village alone. The Prince Bishop of Liege similarly admitted having achieved the paternity of 14 bastards in 22 months. In Germany, the word *Pfaffenkind* (literally, "priest's child") became the commonly used word for any child born out of wedlock.

Of course, many leaders of the Church lamented this scandalous situation. At the Council of Ravenna held in 1261, the presiding archbishop told the parish clergy:

> *I cannot with a safe conscience commit the confessions of the laity to you. . . . For ye lead women behind the altar under pretence of confession and there ye deal as the sons of Eli dealt at the door of the tabernacle, which is horrible to relate and more horrible to do. . . . Can I commit women's confessions to the priest Gerardo here present, when I know well that he has a whole house full of sons and daughters?*

The confession provided a particularly tempting occasion for many a priest. An overwhelming proportion of the sins that women felt compelled to confess were for sexual malfeasance. The priest was obliged to listen to a full description of the erotic act, and to inquire into all the concomitant matters which might modify the rigorousness of the penance.

Such stories or charades—for sometimes an inarticulate girl could only describe what had happened by acting out the occurrence—could be intensely stimulating to the confessor. Attractive penitents who had aroused, beyond recall, the libido of the holy man were often led behind the altar for erotic purpose. The confessional booth was not instituted until the 16th century, and in fact, probably to prevent this very type of church desecration.

Friars, too, at times were called to confess females in private homes, where they enjoyed opportunities far exceeding those in the apocryphal tales of traveling salesmen. Because they were articulate, artful, at ease with strangers, and were moreover considered to have direct access to heaven, priests and friars enjoyed fantastic advantages, and could usually justify or explain away any personal liberties they took.

Many a repressed woman experienced mystical visions of an extremely erotic nature. Mechthild of Magdeburg (1202-1227) often felt God's hand fondling her bosom; Christine Ebner (1277-1356) sincerely believed herself to be with child by Jesus. Religious frenzies occurred frequently; in every case it was necessary to inquire into all the details to determine if the vision was indeed a visitation from God, or a temptation by the Devil, or an instance of witchcraft. Nuns, taught to regard their confessor as a strictly spiritual being, didn't hesitate to reveal to him the most personal details of their lives, sometimes even describing lesbian and bestial intimacies. For many of these offenses, the punishment was flagellation—itself an erotic stimulus of unpredictable effect.

Priests could benefit from hearing the confessions of male sinners as well. An adulterous penitent was nearly always asked the name of his partner in sin, and the priest often promptly inscribed the name into his little black book.

JOHN XXIII ARRIVING AT CONSTANCE   A notoriously immoral man, and one of three contemporary claimants to the Papal throne, John XXIII called the Council of Constance only because of intense pressure from Emperor Sigismund of Bohemia. When he lost control of conciliar proceedings, John fled the city, hoping thereby to force the collapse of the Council.

However, the Council declared its power to be derived not from John but directly from God, and it proceeded to depose the Pope on a number of charges which included atheism, homicide, adultery, and incest.

John was later declared to have been an anti-Pope; his name was stricken from the list of true Popes, so that his style "John XXIII" would be taken by the next true Pope to choose the name of John. However, he had so disgraced the name that for more than 500 years no succeeding Pope chose to be called John. Only in our century did the saintly and widely-loved Angelo Giuseppi Roncalli, elected to the Papacy in 1958, choose to be called "John XXIII," thus redeeming the name.

This illustration, from Ulrich von Richental's "Chronik" of 1417, is preserved in the City Library of Constance.

Euangelium Lucæ am XVI

LIFE AT THE PAPAL COURT
This sixteenth-century copperplate purports to show the dissolute practices of the Pope and his retinue. Undoubtedly exaggerated, it nevertheless illustrates the type of charges leveled against the clerical hierarchy of the day.

Baptism, too, provided temptations. In the early middle ages, converts were baptized naked. By the beginning of the tenth century females were made to wear a single garment of the lightest possible material, which became clingingly transparent when wet. The baptizing priest had to seize the convert by the shoulders and plunge her three times in the water, then anoint her on the forehead, strip off her garment, and wrap her in a robe.

Priests also had the duty to warn girls of the dangers that might result from various gestures. Such descriptions could become vividly graphic. Some were written down; some were acted out. One of the most thorough and lively warnings is found in the Chronicle written by Salimbene di Adamo, a Franciscan monk, born in Parma in 1221. He wrote his chronicle for his 15-year-old niece, who was receiving a convent education. His intent was to warn the girl so that she would never be surprised later in life by the lustful acts of men. His account explains in detail the homosexuality, "especially among scholars and clerks" and also among nuns. Salimbene tells his niece vivid stories of seduction, rape, erotic religious hallucination, blasphemy, and senile lechery. His account records that an aged bishop named Faventino used to take little girls to bed where he fondled them for hours, decorating their most appreciated features with gold coins, which the children were permitted to keep. However, in an appropriately moral ending to the story, old Faventino was finally strangled by a burglar who got his money as well.

Salimbene also tells of one Segarello who started a sect of roving "evangelists." In one incident, three of Segarello's disciples joined a wedding party. Immediately after the ceremony, they took the groom aside and proceeded to get him thoroughly drunk, while one by one, they stole upstairs to "confess" the bride. Segarello, too, got his just deserts; he was burned for heresy in 1300, and his pals were hanged.

Wandering monks and friars too, presented problems as well as values to Christian society. As early as 604, St. Augustine II of England complained of the "hordes of wandering monks, degraded vagrants" who begged, swindled, hawked fake relics, seduced, and hustled in a variety of schemes.

BAPTISM   In this eleventh century drawing, a nubile convert is given the sacrament by priests of the church, sworn to celibacy and to the avoidance of all concupiscent encounters.

IMMERSION   Women and young men could be observed in the nude at baptismal ceremonies.

By the 15th century, a huge volume of tales had grown up, some exaggerated, some quite closely based on truth, concerning the tricks of the wandering friars. Educated and persuasive, these men were supposedly endowed with magical powers. One trick, reported in a tale with several variants, concerns a woman who begged a friar to cure her sterility. He assured her that he could intone a magical chant which would

put her into a trance. In this state, she would believe she was awake and aware of her surroundings, but in reality she would be hallucinating. Then the scoundrel uttered a few talismanic words, after which he raped her. He then uttered another few words to bring her out of her "trance," reassuring her then that everything that she thought had happened was merely a dream. The woman went away, happily believing she had been cured of her sterility. And indeed she had——she bore a child about nine months later.

A similar trick concerned a farmer who asked a friar to stand godfather for his first child, yet unborn. The friar, deeply sympathetic, confided to the farmer that the act of procreation had been incomplete, and that hideously deformed child would be born unless the aid of a third party were engaged to "improve" the fetus. The distressed farmer pleaded with the friar for help. The friar, who had been eying the farmer's pretty young wife, agreed, and unselfishly sacrificed his time, his strength, and his chastity to perform several enthusiastic acts to improve the birth. Subsequently, a perfect child was born, and the young couple were eternally grateful for the friar's miraculous aid.

Another friar showed a young lady his bandaged finger, which he said pained him terribly. A doctor had told him, he said, that the finger would have to be amputated unless it could be placed in a degree of animal heat—for instance, that of a female generative organ—that would dissolve the abscess. As a holy man, of course, he couldn't do any such thing—although if such a deed were done in complete darkness, he said, it would not really be a sin. The sympathetic girl offered her help. The act was carried out in total darkness, and with great care. At the climax, the friar gave a cry of triumph. "Aha!" he cried. "Behold! The abscess has burst and the pus has escaped! I am cured."

Many other tales indicate the temper of Europe in those days. Ribald lyrics composed by wandering friars and clerics, were ofttimes written in hymn meters and dealt with riotous subject matter, reflecting the clerical preoccupation. A large body of these songs, the famous *Carmina Burana,* were later found in a Bavarian abbey of the Benedictines, and date back to the 12th and 13th centuries.

Educated women also wrote lively tales. The 10th cen-

ROVING HANDS   *This miniature from a fourteenth-century Bible depicts some monks and their lady friends in the monastery kitchen.*

ORGY IN A MONASTERY   Revels of the monks, as shown in a
sixteenth - century Dutch drawing.

tury German nun, Hrotswitha, wrote a number of plays in
Latin. Some of her scenes are set in brothels; one, in a ceme-
tery, where a lover digs up his mistress's corpse to abuse it.

In one riotous comedy, Hrotswitha depicts a pagan Roman

general who is tricked by magical art into fondling pots and pans, under the delusion that they are Christian virgins he has captured. The virgins watch him from behind a curtain and they giggle. When he discovers the hoax, he furiously plans an orgy with the captured virgins. But as his soldiers try to strip the girls, the clothes simply won't come off. By a miracle of God, as soon as the clothes are pulled down, they slide up again.

Indeed, the nunneries provided a whole range of scandal. The early nunneries served as schools for the daughters of gentlemen. These institutions had to be respectable enough to please protective fathers, and yet not too strict, else the girls would refuse to go. In the convents, schoolgirls were educated and prepared for marriages appropriate to their station in life. The convents also provided a convenient dumping ground for orphans, cripples, old maids, or girls who otherwise did not fit well into the social scheme. Some girls were forced into convents by their relatives, either for status or for riddance. In 1359, one such German girl composed the following stanzas:

> *God give him a year of blight*
> *Who made me to be a nun;*
> *Who bade me take this tunic white*
> *And this coal-black mantle don.*

> *And must I be a nun in truth*
> *And all against my will;*
> *When I could cool a lad's hot youth*
> *And all his passion still?*

Such girls apparently were not cut out for sainthood.

Charges that convents were being used as brothels kept recurring constantly. As early as the eighth century, King Ethelbald of Mercia regularly used the Anglo-Saxon nunneries for this purpose, and was regularly rebuked by St. Boniface for this habit.

In 836, the Council of Aix-la-Chapelle openly declared that many abbesses were to blame for running their convents as bawdy-houses. The Council directed future architects to be sure that there would be no "dark corners" in convents that could be used for immoral purposes.

About 650 years later, in 1489, the Prioress of Appleton in Yorkshire received a similar warning, and was directed not to let the sisters continue to hang around the alehouse or to bathe at the "watersyde where strangers dayly resorte." In those days, outdoor bathing was always in the nude.

The 14th century English author William Langland wrote that "Dame Purnell, a priest's concubine, will never become prioress . . . for she had a child in cherry time, all our Chapter it wist."

TAKING A BATH   According to this fifteenth-century illustration, the delights of mixed bathing were not incompatible with the monastic life. This picture and the accompanying manuscripts, the Jena Codex, are preserved today in the Prague National Museum of Czechoslovakia.

Other ambitious girls, however, did forge ahead by such means. In 1489, the Archbishop of Canterbury charged the Abbot of St. Albans with appointing a whore named Elena Germyn as his prioress, and with sharing her favors with any of his monks who desired to partake of the lady's charms. Looking back on this period, the scholar Erasmus wrote that chastity was more endangered in the cloister than out of it; and Thomas Fuller philosophically mused that "Virginity is least kept where it is most constrained." It was true. Abbots and their staffs would often call on Abesses and their staffs— supposedly to discuss ecclesiastical matters. Many such meetings were followed by overnight wild parties.

ALTAR CARVING   This picture of a lascivious monk and nun was carved in bas-relief on an altar in the Cathedral of Notre Dame in Strasbourg, a church unfortunately destroyed in the eighteenth century.

Upon the dissolution of the convents in England under Henry VIII (1491-1547) the bones of newborn babies were found "all over the place," in convents, for it was much more difficult for nuns than for priests to get their bastards accepted in the outside world. This widespread infanticide is even more noteworthy in light of the penalties in effect at that time. Since a child who died unbaptized was condemned to everlasting perdition, a convicted mother was usually burned or buried alive.

During the 10th century, loose federations of monks and nuns were established which led to the building of "double monasteries" with only a wall between monks and nuns. This innovation was notoriously unsuccessful, nearly all the nuns becoming pregnant.

The isolation of the convents exacted its psychological toll. Though the orders tried to keep their inmates busy through study and work, the libido chafed. Balzac writes that the nuns of Poissy were particularly renowned as lesbians; they had worked out a successful system of being able to eat their cake and have it too, for they believed that the important thing in heaven's eyes was to retain their virginity from being despoiled by males.

Other nuns kept pets. Canines could easily be trained either for tongue work or for actual copulation; other animals were also occasionally implicated. How widespread the practice was can be gathered from the fact certain convents prohibited the entry of specified animals.

Demonology also provided a good excuse for sexual license. It was believed that succubi, or female demons, would jump into bed with the most devout priest or monk, and try his chastity to the utmost. There were also incubi, demons shaped like handsome young men with magnificent physical endowments, who would interrupt the sleep of a nun or an Abbess. In 1491, Jeanne Pothiere, a nun of Cambrai, swore that such

DISCIPLINARY MEASURES   *"In the cloister garden, there is such punishment as here is shown," reads the inscription on this bawdy engraving by M. Greuber, whose clear intent is to lampoon the sanctimonious lechery of the monks.*

a demon had forced her to copulate with him 444 times. Furthermore, he had demanded that she introduce him to her sisters in Christ; and he had then chased the nuns around the fields and yards and up into trees.

Possession by a demon proved to be a good excuse to let off steam. Epidemics of hysteria swept nunnery after nunnery. When a woman was "possessed," she was clearly not herself, and therefore could not be blamed for anything she might do. So in such seizures, the sisters would roll on the floor,

pull up their skirts, show their private parts, use foul language, make obscene gestures, and invite sex. Even the crucifix was employed as a phallus. By their lewd behavior, nuns in the throes undoubtedly invited raids by men of the surrounding area. It was generally found that oratory had no effect on a "possessed" person. Exorcism was more effective, especially when accompanied by copious doses of ice-water, resounding slaps, and painful limb-twisting which encouraged a nun to snap out of her demoniacal state.

Nunneries were frequently stormed by goons. In 1379, the brutish soldier John Arundel, on his way to war against France, kidnapped 60 women and girls from a convent near Southampton. Aboard his ships in the channel, his soldiers were raping the captives when a violent storm arose. To lighten the periously overloaded ships, the women were thrown overboard. There is no record of any punishment ever having been meted out to Sir John for his chivalry.

The medieval church was also indirectly responsible for other scandalous customs. A man would join a Crusade, leave his home for years at a time, expecting his wife to be faithful. Fidelity was sometimes enforced by the husband encasing his spouse in a chastity belt. Often, though, wives and their lovers made duplicate keys, or circumvented the husband's interdiction by some other means. In many cases, clerics became involved as comforters of lonely and abandoned wives.

The Crusades also saw the establishment of military orders for men: the Hospitallers, Templars, and Teutonic Knights. Both on their military missions and at home, these groups cultivated male comradeship, and spurned the supposedly corrupting influence of women. The rampant homosexuality rife in these quasi-religious orders became a scandal of the day.

A GIFT FROM HUBBY   About to embark upon a Crusade for his Church, a medieval nobleman presents his wife with a chastity belt. It is uncertain whether he mainly distrusts his wife or he rather distrusts the clergy who remained behind and would comfort her in her loneliness.

During the Crusades, Egyptian and Moorish female slaves captured in battle were sold throughout Western Europe—even to priests.

Another custom of the medieval period was the so-called "right of the first night" (*jus primae noctis*) whereby the lord of a manor under his "droit de seigneur" could enjoy a bride on the first night of her marriage, even before the husband had carnal knowledge of his wife. This right was often exercised by clerical higher-ups, and a few monasteries made this a steady practice. All brides-to-be, married under the auspices of such an institution, were required to make their pilgrimage to the monastery, there to be deflowered. In some localities, it was customary for the bride to bring a gift to the cleric who was scheduled to take her virginity.

The medieval church also drew attacks for its financial rapacity. Saddled with its many hierarchical dependents, and also with costly special projects such as the construction of St. Peter's Church in Rome, the Roman Church felt constrained to raise money by dubious or even by corrupt means. To finance its works and its enormous hierarchy, the church imposed grievous taxes: for example, in the 14th century, England paid five times as much money by a variety of means: through the sale of indulgences, through obligatory confession, through baptismal, nuptial and funeral fees, through appointments to ecclesiastical office, and through hundreds of other transactions.

Among many other high-placed prelates, Cardinal Wolsey stunned his observers with his sartorial magnificence—especially his fashionable tight pants which revealed every curve and angle of his body. As early as the seventh century, Aldheim, Bishop of Sherborne, complained of

> *the bold impudence and conceit of nuns who wear*
> *a vest of linen dyed violet and over it a scarlet tunic*

with a hood, the sleeves striped with silk and trim-
med with red fur. Their locks, on forehead and
temples, are curled with a crisping-iron. They have
white and colored headgear with bows of ribbon
reaching to the ground. Their finger-nails are pared
till they resemble the talons of a hawk.

Similar descriptions appear in other accounts throughout the Middle Ages.

Simony, the selling of church offices, was one of the chief scandals of the day. Abbeys, bishoprics,, and even arch-bishoprics went to the highest bidder. Simony was especially blatant in Germany where high Church office often brought the purchaser vast tracts of land to exploit. Germany's prince-ly houses vied with one another for the chairs of important prelates, and the Papacy adroitly played off one house against the other until ducats and guilders flew over the Alps in enor-mous sums. Even boys were made bishops and abbots through the influence of friends and relatives who expected to profit handsomely from their investments. Many of the churchmen who acquired office through financial or political deals were extremely worldly-minded and self-seeking men. Once estab-lished in their churchly offices, they tended to consider their positions as conferring personal prerogatives. Bishops in Ger-many, in blatant disregard of the rules of priestly celibacy, often married and passed their bishoprics on to their sons.

A practice even more coldheartedly calculating was the selling of indulgences. It was this vile traffic that scandalized Martin Luther, then an obscure Augutinian monk of Saxony, and finally led to the Reformation and the Protestant schism from Rome. So many pennies given to the Church would purchase for the ignorant so many days' release from pur-gatory—a condonation of transgression bought like so much merchandise in a store. One could literally buy his way out

TRAFFIC IN REDEMPTION   A rare engraving by Hans Holbein depicts indulgence transactions in the sixteenth century.

MONEY-CHANGERS RESTORED TO POWER   *The Protestant engraver Lucas Cranach depicts Christ driving the money-lenders out of the Temple, and the Pope bringing the money-lenders back in, through the Papal edicts and the church sale of indulgences. The pictures are from Cranach's 1521 series entitled "The Passion of Christ and Anti-Christ," with accompanying text by Luther's noted follower Melanchthon.*

SALE OF INDULGENCES   *A German woodcut depicts
the sale of letters of indulgence in a German market place at
the time of Luther. Indulgences were a particularly controversial issue in Germany at this time. Upon receipt of a substantial payment, Pope Leo X had granted permission to
Albrecht of Brandenburg to simultaneously hold three lucrative bishoprics and enjoy the revenue from each of them. To
pay off his bribe to the Pope, Albrecht needed cash. Since the
German churchman received a 50% cut on all indulgences sold
in his territory, Albrecht naturally pushed sales. To this purpose, he imported John Tetzel and other skillful hucksters.*

of Hell. There was a theological justification for the sale of indulgences: it was held that the pope possessed a treasury of the superfluous merits accumulated by the saints, and that he had unlimited dispensation of these credits. Indulgences, then, would be sold in the form of a document transferring certain credits to the purchaser's account.

DOCUMENT   *A plenary indulgence printed by Gutenberg in 1455.*

TETZEL: SUPER SALESMAN   *One of the most crassly commercial of the*
indulgence peddlers, John Tetzel used a variety of merchandising techniques to

*market God's forgiveness. He is shown here with his panoply and his sales assistants.
The engraving is by R. Brendamour, from an original drawing by Haeberlin.*

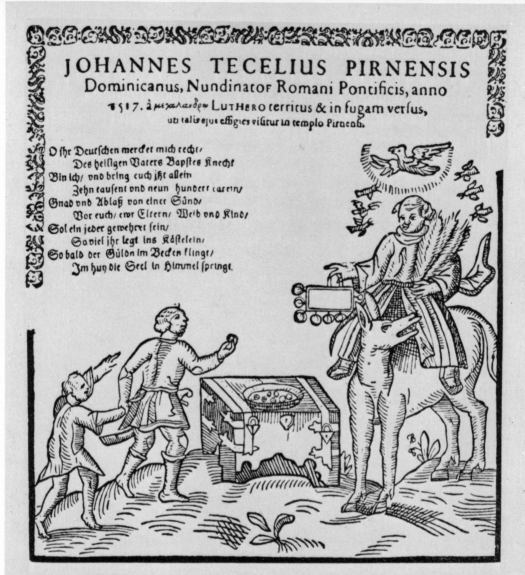

JOHANNES TECELIUS PIRNENSIS

Dominicanus, Nundinator Romani Pontificis, anno
1517. à μεγαλανδρω LUTHERO territus & in fugam versus,
uti talis ejus effigies visitur in templo Pirneñ.

O Ihr Deutschen merket mich recht/
    Des heiligen Vaters Bapstes Knecht
Bin Ich/ vnd bring euch itzt allein
    Zehn tausent vnd neun hundert carein/
Gnad vnd Ablaß von einer Sünd/
    Vor euch/ ewr Eltern/ Weib vnd Kind/
Sol ein jeder gewehret sein/
    Soviel ihr legt ins Kästelein/
So bald der Gülden im Becken klingt/
    Im huy die Seel in Himmel springt.

Zeitgenössisches Flugblatt auf den Ablaßhandel Tetzels.

HANDBILL ADVERTISING INDULGENCES   This 1517 broadsheet promoted the wares of John Tetzel, the most noted or notorious seller of indulgences during the time of Luther. In rhythms suggestive of our singing commercials today, the German jingle presented Tetzel's offer: "Oh you Germans, pay me proper attention. I am the servant of the Holy Papal Father. I bring 10,900 indulgences. I bring mercy and pardon from sin, for you, your parents, your wife and child. Everyone who buys these will be as well protected as if he lived securely in a castle. As soon as the money clinks in the basin, the soul springs up to Heaven."

The across-the-counter sale of indulgences went hand in hand with the veneration of holy relics. In the church of the Electors of Saxony, there were almost 18,000 relics. There was a tear that Jesus had shed when he wept over the recalcitrance of Jerusalem; there was a twig from the burning bush of Moses. Pilgrims came from miles around to gain benefit from these relics; for by making the appropriate prayers and by contributing the appropriate offerings, even the worst of sinners could earn remission for as many as 1,902,-202 years in purgatory.

Luther was outraged, and declared,

> *What shall I say of such as cry up and maintain the cheat of pardons and indulgences? that by these cheats compute the time of each soul's residence in purgatory, and assign them a longer or shorter residence there, according as they purchase more or fewer of these paltry pardons? . . . By this way of purchasing pardons, any notorious highwayman, any plundering soldier, any bribe-taking judge, shall gain exemption for some part of their unjust gains, and think all their grossest impieties atoned for; so many perjuries, lusts, drunkennesses, quarrels, bloodsheds, cheats, treacheries, and all sorts of debaucheries, shall all be, as it were, struck a bargain for. . . .*

Addressing himself to Pope Leo X, Luther ranted against Rome, with justification or without, depending upon one's viewpoint.

> *(It) is clearer than the day to all men . . . (that) the Roman Church, once the most holy of all, has become the most licentious den of thieves, the most shameless of all brothels, the kingdom of sin, death,*

·

MARTIN LUTHER   Whether or not one agrees with his teachings, one must concede that Luther is one of the few men who have profoundly altered the history of the world.

The son of a peasant miner, Luther had studied for the law. However, a narrow escape from being struck by lightning, along with a period of deep contemplation after the death of a friend, led Luther to enter the German Congregation of the Augustinians in 1505. This order, which had been thoroughly reformed shortly before Luther's time, embodied most of the best traditions of medieval monasticism.

Luther became a professor at the University of Wittenberg, which had been founded in 1502 by the Saxon Elector, Frederick the Wise. However, despite his learning and his monastic piety, Luther still lacked peace of soul. He became convinced that salvation depended not on the adding up of a man's works or of his contributions, but depended solely on his faith, which could place him in a new relationship with God. Upon this realization, Luther experienced what he considered to be a profound religious revelation which gave him the courage to face the trials ahead.

After the posting of his Ninety-Five Theses in 1517 controversy grew thick and fast. Standing before the Emperor and the Reichstag at the Diet of Worms, Luther refused to recant, uttering his now famous words: "Here I stand. I can do no other. God help me. Amen."

While clerics and emperor condemned him, the German nobility were impressed with his ideas. The protection of powerful Germans, among whom the Elector Frederick was the most notable, saved him from a prompt and bloody martyrdom.

Along with his catalytic impact upon the history of Christianity, Luther also exercised great influence upon the development of the German language. His accurate, idiomatic, and readable translation of the Bible largely determined the form of speech that was to mark future German literature.

This portrait was painted by Lucas Cranach the Elder, who was called to Frederick's court in 1505 and who then became a follower of Luther. The picture was completed in 1540, six years before Luther's death.

LUTHER'S NINETY-FIVE THESES   At Wittenberg, Germany, on October 31, 1517, Martin Luther's Ninety-Five Theses were nailed to the door of the castle church, which served as the University bulletin board. The posting of such statements was the customary manner of raising issues for academic debate.

In his Theses, Luther protested abuses in the church, particularly the sale of indulgences. Luther's Theses did not attack the church as a whole; he did not intend a break with Rome. However, the ensuing accusations of heresy leveled against him, finally drove him to choose between his church and his convictions. He refused to recant, and was excommunicated. But popular feeling and German nationalism concurred in his support, and thus led to the establishment of the new Protestant church.

This drawing shows Luther in the left foreground, discussing the issues with another member of his Order, while a young assistant nails up the Theses.

and hell; so that even Antichrist himself, should he come, could think of nothing to add to its wickedness.

Partly in response to such criticisms as these, the Church

instituted a series of reforms, which have come to be known
in history as the Counter-Reformation. In the following years,
the Council of Trent, held in 1545, reaffirmed basic Catholic
doctrine but called for reforms within the Church. A major
statement by the Council called for "frugality, modesty, con-

tinency, and . . . holy humility" on the part of Cardinals and all prelates of the churches; it encouraged them to "be content with modest furniture and a frugal table," and "not enrich their relatives or domestics out of the property of the Church." Another major statement covered indulgences, and insisted that "moderation be observed," rather than "excessive facility." All bishops were then instructed to collect, evidences of any abuses, and to report them to the provincial Synods.

The statements, of course, tacitly admitted the abuses.

THE PERFIDY OF ALFRED REDL

There has perhaps been only one traitor in this century without a single saving grace. He was Colonel Alfred Redl, head of the Operations Section of the Intelligence Bureau of the Austro-Hungarian Empire before World War I. Redl was the ultimate in traitors. No flicker of ideology or misguided patriotism redeemed his treason. His homosexual lust and his need for the money with which to gratify it were the only reasons for one of the greatest betrayals in history.

Alfred Victor Redl was born in 1864 in the town of Lemberg (now Lvov in the Ukraine). His father had once held a commission as a lieutenant in the Imperial Army; he now worked on the railway as an ill-paid freight clerk. Alfred was one of nine hungry children, made even hungrier by the death of his father. His widowed mother was left without any money, except for a marginal railway pension. Persons of a psychoanalytical bent might well have a field day with this information, since Redl's childhood undoubtedly contributed massively to his homosexual inclinations, and was partly responsible for the cold rage with which he viewed his coevals, and which allowed him to betray his country, his associates, and eventually himself with perfect ease and facility. His career has about it an ambience of childishness; an unutterably angry child, lost and pathetic, who stands behind the facade of a thoroughly evil and conscienceless adult.

Unfortunately perhaps, his father's previous commission in

the army had left a partially open doorway to a future for young Alfred. Cadet school and an officer's education were free to an officer's son; and in 1877, at the age of fourteen, he became a cadet officer.

At cadet school, Redl was introduced to homosexuality. Within a short time, abnormal practices became his driving force, and his sexual nature was fixed for the rest of his life.

He joined the Austrian Imperial Army in 1881 and was commissioned in 1887. The routine was empty and monotonous. The officers were underpaid, and only those with private incomes or wealthy parents avoided getting into debt.

Outwardly Redl pretended to pursue women, but secretly, he had affairs with men. He had learned early to spot abnormality among his fellow officers. Whatever its drawbacks, overt invasion was the cheapest way of obtaining sex for an impoverished officer.

Redl's one attempt at a normal sexual relationship failed miserably. He fell in love with a pretty circus performer, and even thought of marrying her. But when she gave him syphilis, he was forever finished with women. The treatment for syphilis at that time was painful and nauseating, and he was never completely cured.

In the army of that time, venereal disease was as common as a toothache and as universally accepted. Its appearance in Redl's medical reports made an effective smoke screen for his real sex life, and provided sufficient reason for the fact that he never married.

Syphilis was no bar, either, to candidacy for a position on the Imperial General Staff. The course of study, which lasted two years, was very difficult, both physically and academically. It was not unusual for students to commit suicide, so difficult was it to pass the course and gain a position on the General Staff.

Redl, however, had no trouble. He was a highly intelligent

ALFRED VICTOR REDL In full dress uniform, Redl displays the medals awarded him by his unsuspecting country.

young pederast with overpowering ambition. He graduated successfully in 1894 and joined the Austrian Imperial General Staff, whose officers were considered superior to those of the Prussian General Staff.

Life seemed good. He was stationed in Vienna where existence in the 1890s was gay and pleasant. He quickly earned a reputation for elegance and good manners. His clothes were always impeccable, his uniforms models of perfection. His one disadvantage was that he was short—a mere 5 feet 3 inches, with broad shoulders and slim hips. But this was not necessarily a disadvantage. He had presence and personality and was highly thought of by his superiors, who regarded him as a first-class officer.

His stature was no disadvantage to his secret love life either. Since his syphilis seemed to have disappeared, he pursued his homosexual affairs ardently. Actually the disease was just in a quiescent period.

Redl spent four years savoring his own peculiar pleasures and wrestling with the mounting debts which they brought in their train. Then it was suggested to him that his talents could best be used by the Intelligence Bureau. He found the prospect interesting and was sent to Russia on an exchange basis to perfect his knowledge of Russian. Nineteenth century intelligence was carried on mostly through the respective embassies and was regarded as a gentleman's business. In both Russia and the Austro-Hungarian Empire, the monarchs of each country had the final say in such matters as an exchange between General Staff Officers "for cultural reasons."

Russia, then as now, was riddled with secret police. Ochrana, the Russian Secret Service, spent most of its time and energy in keeping the Russian revolutionaries in check. With what was left, they kept their eye on their neighbors. Although the Tsar's General Staff would not countenance such ungentlemanly conduct as espionage, Ochrana was well aware that the two officers sent every year to Russia by the Austrian General Staff were in training for the Intelligence Bureau in Vienna. As for the Austrian Intelligence Bureau, it wished, despite the Emperor's frown, to strengthen its espionage activities against Russia, which was constantly becoming more of a military threat to the Austro-Hungarian Empire.

During their stay in Russia, Captain Redl and his companion Captain Dani were under constant observation by Ochrana. Redl's homosexual activities were already surmised by Ochrana. To test the validity of their suspicions, they indulged in a most naive and unsubtle maneuver. They dispatched one of their most alluring female agents to seduce him. When he declined to sleep with the girl their suspicions were confirmed, and they wrote him down as an easy subject for future blackmail. Redl was well aware of this latter danger and he was extremely cautious about indulging his sexual whims while in Russia.

His syphilis became active again during his Russian stay. The doctor he consulted told him it was in the tertiary stage. He went to a sanatorium to receive mercury treatments. Ochrana soon discovered the nature of his illness, which they regarded as one of the best jokes of the decade. Here indeed was a gentleman, a veritable cavalier, who had refused to infect a beautiful female agent. They sent him flowers in the girl's name, wishing him a speedy recovery from the fever which had overwhelmed him. However, they did not forget him.

In 1900 he returned to Vienna with the highest qualifications. Now fluent in Russian, he was appointed to the Intelligence Bureau of the General Staff of the Imperial Army, the head of which was General Baron von Giesl. Von Giesl thought highly of Redl and he appointed him Chief of the Russian Section and also Chief of the Operations Section.

Intelligence was obtained then (as it is now, for the most part) from a perceptive study of foreign newspapers and military journals, and from the reports sent in by the agents and military attachés of various foreign embassies.

Redl was quick to see that the Operations Section was the

FELLOW OFFICERS A group of Austro-Hungarian officers of the Kaiserlich-Koeniglich summoned up their full military dignity for the cameraman. Redl stands at extreme left in the third row.

key section which, if efficiently developed, could control the Intelligence Bureau and place him in a position of great power. He persuaded von Giesl to relieve him of his work in the Russian Section and allow him to concentrate on his role as Chief of Operations. Von Giesl was well aware of the weakness of the Intelligence Bureau and knew that Redl was able to pinpoint specific problems. Therefore, von Giesl backed him to the hilt.

Redl's work in the Austrian Intelligence Bureau was brilliant. Under his dynamic and far-seeing leadership it became the most efficient and up-to-date secret service then in existence. Von Giesl considered him a genius, although the highest echelons of the Imperial Army still felt that espionage was no occupation for a gentleman. The Austrian Foreign Office particularly despised the Intelligence Bureau.

Redl, consumed by his work, labored long hours and took little time off. Such private life as he had was very private indeed. He acquired a handsome seventeen-year-old, named Joseph, who acted as his servant by day, and, dressed as a girl, as his pathic by night. Naturally, Joseph was highly paid for his services.

But Ochrana's memory was long. Redl's successful activities in the Intelligence Bureau had been highly embarrassing to the Russian Intelligence Service, particularly to Colonel Nikolai Stepanovitch Batjuschin. Batjuschin was the Chief of the West Russian Espionage Center, whose headquarters were in Warsaw, which was then in Russia, since there was no independent state of Poland.

Batjuschin's agents watched Redl day and night, and soon came to the conclusion that their continuing suspicions of him were correct. One of them rented the apartment underneath his and "tapped" Redl's bedroom with a piece of pipe. These were the days before microphones, but the pipe apparently worked well enough to allow the agent to hear some highly compromising conversations between Redl and his lovers.

The Russian agents then confronted Redl with the fact that they had sufficient proof of his homosexual activities to ruin him. They made Redl an offer. If he would provide them with the information to which he had access in the course of his intelligence duties, they would not betray his secret. They would also pay him handsomely, and he would not only be able to pay his debts but be able to pursue his expensive inclinations to his heart's content.

OUT FOR A RIDE   Social call—or spying mission? His destination a mystery, Redl rides with another officer in an open carriage.

It was a subtle and clever offer. A harsh blackmail threat might have made Redl confess the truth to von Giesl, who might in turn have been sufficiently sympathetic to arrange a transfer for Redl to a remote corner of the Empire. But the large sums of money which the Russians promised, plus the fact that to them his homosexuality was little more than a joke, made all the difference to Alfred Redl.

To Redl, his country came a long way down the list of the things he loved. And it is true enough that patriotism was not a strong element in Francis Joseph's disorderly jumble of an empire, with its patchwork of nationalities which included Czechs, Hungarians, Slavs, Italians, Austrians, Poles and Croats. Redl's treason must be judged in context: Austria-Hungary was not a nation, but a collection of rebellious peoples held together by force and ruled by the hated Hapsburgs. It was a ramshackle empire for which few felt any loyalty, and which fell to pieces of its own accord at the end of World War I.

This only partially explains Redl's enormous treason. The rest was lust and greed.

Then began one of the greatest treacheries in the history of espionage. Redl had no scruples whatsoever. He gave the Russians more than they demanded. He betrayed his own agents, spies acting under his own instructions to them. In return the Russians gaily betrayed some of their spies to him, for it was in their own interests that Redl should retain his reputation in the Austrian Intelligence Bureau. During this time Redl's ability became widely respected. Honors were showered upon him.

Treason was a profitable thing. The Russians paid him handsomely, many times more than his army pay. He was not above moonlighting and gaily sold Austria's secrets to France and Italy as well.

He explained his sudden wealth by saying that he had inher-

LT. COLONEL MAXIMILIAN RONGE   Formerly Redl's student
in the arts of espionage, Ronge learned so well that he succeeded in
unmasking the traitorous Redl.

ARTHUR FREIHERR VON GIESL-GIESLINGEN Head of the Intelligence Bureau of the General Staff of the Imperial Army in Vienna, Baron von Giesl thought highly of Redl and appointed him to positions of power.

ited a fortune from an old uncle who had just died in Galacia. And, of course, no one doubted the word of an officer and a gentleman.

He pursued his sex life with avid caution. His main sweetheart was a handsome young cadet named Stefan Hromodka, for whom Redl pulled the right strings in order to get him into the Wiener Neustadt Academy. He posed as the youth's uncle, and seduced him during a holiday on the Dalmatian Coast. Stefan, while not actively homosexual, accommodated himself readily to Redl's desires. Redl made him an allowance and gave him gifts.

In 1909, with war clouds on the European horizon, there arose a greater degree of cooperation between the Austrian and German intelligence systems. Redl went to northern France and England to reconnoiter railway systems there. In Berlin he held an important conference with the Chief of German intelligence. In those days there was a continuous threat of war in the Balkans, since Serbia and Austria were hurling threats and counter-threats at each other. The Austrian General Staff made out a detailed plan for the invasion of Serbia, and Redl sold this plan to Russia, Serbia's ally.

A Russian plan for attacking Germany and Austria came into his possession through a defecting Russian who was ignorant of Redl's own treachery. Redl betrayed the defector to the Russians, returned their plans to them, and drew up phony plans which he gave to his own superiors.

The Balkan crisis had been responsible for a considerable expansion of the Viennese Intelligence Bureau. One of Redl's brightest pupils was Captain Max Ronge—who was later to be responsible for Redl's downfall and death. There were moves to make Redl head of the Bureau, but although he dominated it, he never became its head. The man destined to be its chief was a colonel on the General Staff named Urbanski, who was also in at the death when Redl was finally caught. Redl, blind to all irony, was silently and sincerely furious that Urbanski was preferred to him.

Through all these dangerous activities (for he was constantly in touch with the intelligence services of countries which were potential enemies) he continued his affair with Stefan Hromodka, now a second lieutenant conveniently posted near Vienna through Redl's influence. No one thought there was anything wrong with a handsome young officer spending nights in his uncle's apartment. Stefan always referred to Redl as his rich uncle, and he was not enthusiastic enough about homosexual practices to indulge in them with anyone else. He permitted Redl to make love to him because he got so much out of it. Redl was paying him fifty crowns a month, and was continually warning him of the dangers of having anything to do with women.

Later Redl arranged for Stefan to go to an exclusive cavalry regiment which consisted only of officers with private incomes. He increased the young man's salary and bought him a car. Redl himself drove around in a smart Austro-Daimler, which was the envy of the General Staff. Life was good. The only trouble was that Stefan kept threatening to leave him and get married, and Redl had to increase his allowance and make him expensive presents in order to retain his affections. He was eventually to pay Stefan 600 crowns a month, which was more than his own salary as colonel; a rank he attained in 1911.

He was transferred from the Intelligence Bureau and made a regimental commander. He was awarded a medal and received a personal citation from the Emperor for his services. In 1912 he became General Staff Chief of the Eighth Corps in Prague. There was no intelligence department in Prague but Redl's connections with the Vienna Intelligence Bureau gave him legitimate access to the Imperial Army's secrets; secrets which he continued to sell to Russia, France and Italy.

He certainly needed the money now, for he was living at a fantastic rate. Stefan's demands on him became more and more exorbitant. A glutton for punishment, he had other male lovers, some of whom were blackmailing him.

In his apartments near the Staff Headquarters at Prague was a room to which only himself and his personal servant had the key. It contained an enormous four-poster bed, and besides his 195 dress shirts, 10 uniform silk-lined greatcoats, 25 pairs of uniform trousers and 400 suede golves, there were also women's kimonos, blouses and silk stockings and shoes.

But no women ever entered the place. Only his servant and

certain handsome young officers shared his transvestite revels. He took numerous obscene photographs of himself and his lovers. He built up a large collection of homosexual pornography. These pictures he kept in the same locked desk where he kept the photographic equipment with which he photographed the secret documents he sent to Russia.

Meanwhile, Major Ronge, faithfully following Redl's methods in Vienna, established a strict postal censorship. In April, 1913, he intercepted two mysterious envelopes containing 14,000 crowns, the equivalent of $3500.00, but with no covering letters. They were addressed to a post office box in Vienna.

Ronge was almost certain that this money was espionage payment, and he knew it was just a matter of waiting until the guilty party came to collect it.

His agents had to wait six weeks, and by the time their man turned up for the envelopes their enthusiasm had worn thin, their patience was exhausted, and Redl nearly got away.

One detective phoned Ronge, while the other followed Redl's taxi. Redl went to the Hotel Klomser. The detectives meanwhile found the cab he had used and in it a pocket knife which Redl had carelessly dropped while he was opening his envelopes. This knife, given to him by Stefan Hromodka, was destined to be fatal to him, for the detectives just handed it to the desk clerk, and told him to ask each of the hotel guests if it belonged to him.

Why Redl fell into the trap of admitting it was his we shall never know. He suspected he was being followed. He must have lost his touch.

The detectives knew him well enough, as did the desk clerk, and when the detectives heard him admit the knife was his, they could hardly believe their ears. He left the hotel in a hurry, followed by one of the detectives, while the other telephoned Ronge.

Ronge did not permit the fantastic news to shock him into a state of inaction. He immediately got in touch with Colonel Urbanski, now Chief of Intelligence, and General Conrad von Hotzendorf, Chief of the General Staff, and told them that the traitor they had been seeking was Redl. Hotzendorf, who had had a high opinion of Redl and had been pushing his career for some time, was devastated; and when he thought of all that he had done for Redl, his sense of shock turned to cold fury. He ordered the matter kept absolutely secret and he ordered Redl's death.

Redl made no attempt to escape. He knew it would be useless. He was finished. There would be no mercy for him. He retired to his room at the Hotel Klomser and contemplated methods of suicide. It was useless now to think of the mistakes which had led to his downfall; going to the post office openly to collect his letters; opening the letters in the taxi with the knife Stefan had given him; admitting ownership of the knife. He had been too confident. Years of getting away with it had been responsible for this. Well, now it was the end. He would just have to wait until they came for him.

At half past midnight there was a knock on his door. Four officers stood outside. Redl let them in. They included Urbanski and Ronge.

"I know why you have come," said Redl immediately. "I would like to speak to Major Ronge alone."

They left him alone with Ronge. He begged Ronge for a pistol with which to shoot himself. Ronge went to his senior officer outside and permission was given for Redl's suicide.

Urbanski asked Redl whom he had worked for, who were his accomplices and how much of his country's secrets he had betrayed. Redl did not give a completely truthful answer to any of these questions, except to say he had no accomplices. "Only a fool uses accomplices," he said. He added: "You will find the answer to everything in my desk in Prague."

REDL'S STUDY "*You will find the answer to everything in my desk at Prague,*" *Redl told his arresting officers. In this locked desk, investigators found massive evidence of Redl's treason, and an astounding collection of homosexual pornography, some of which showed other army officers in compromising poses.*

This drawing also shows some of the photographic and recording equipment which Redl used.

They gave him his pistol and left him alone. He wrote an unconscionable number of letters, while the four officers waited outside the hotel for the sound which would tell them of his death. They had to wait till four-thirty, and became very impatient. They finally heard the shot and went away.

A few minutes later the night porter at the Klomser received a call from Army Headquarters, requesting him to bring Colonel Redl to the phone immediately on urgent business. The porter went to the room and found Redl lying in a pool of blood, dead, a pistol beside him. He rushed to the phone with the news, but the caller had hung up.

At first the authorities tried to keep the scandal quiet, to pass it off as an ordinary suicide. Urbanski made an inspection of Redl's apartment in Prague and was profoundly shocked, not only at the extent of the treason which was revealed, but at the obscenity of the homosexual photographs which served to betray not only Redl's perversion, but also that of other officers of the Imperial Army.

It was impossible to keep the mess quiet for long. The story leaked into foreign newspapers and became the talk of Vienna. The shock was tremendous, particularly since the sole reason for Redl's treason was to obtain financing for his homosexual affairs.

Questions were asked in the Austrian Parliament. There was much criticism of the army for allowing Redl to shoot himself, thus rendering a full investigation into the affair impossible. The Archduke Francis Ferdinand—whose murder at Sarajevo a year later was to spark off World War I—was particularly indignant, on religious grounds, at the fact that suicide was more or less forced upon Redl.

The whole affair was a terrible blow to the Austrian Army and was the cause of widespread recrimination, horror and disgust. It ruined the good relations between the Austrian and German General Staffs. Von Moltke no longer trusted the

Austrians, and the two allies entered the war in 1914 in a state of mutual disaffection.

Anti-semitism was strong in Europe in those days. An unknown Cardinal at the Vatican blamed the incident on the international machinations of the Jews, saying that Redl was a Jew, and that his real name was Redlich. The Austrian authorities seriously investigated this claim and found no Jewish blood at all in Redl.

Stefan Hromodka was arrested and tried for unnatural prostitution. He received the relatively mild sentence of three months' hard labor. He was dishonorably dismissed from the army with ignominy, after which he married and began a new life.

The result of Redl's treachery was to be truly felt only when war came. He had betrayed to Russia the Austrian High Command's plan for the invasion of Serbia, and the Russians passed on the information to the Serbian High Command. Early in the war Austria sustained terrible defeats at the hands of both Serbia and Russia. Some authorities state that a quarter of a million men of the Imperial Army died on the field of battle because of Redl's treason. In 1915, a hundred and twenty secret Austrian and German documents were found in Russian Intelligence Headquarters in Warsaw, and it is believed that Redl was responsible for a large portion of them.

The Austro-Hungarian Empire was nearing its inglorious end. Alfred Redl's infamy pushed it one step nearer its doom.

ATROCITIES OF THE BELGIAN CONGO

In the 19th century, the Congo was an abundant land, its estimated 25 million inhabitants were, by and large, a relatively happy people. They were peaceful and industrious, and lived in pastoral simplicity. If occasionally they were intruded upon by Arab slave traders, the tenor of their ways was not vitally disturbed; slave traders had been with them for centuries.

In 1876, King Leopold II of Belgium, eyeing the Congo as a lush territory ripe for exploitation, proclaimed the formation of an International African Association, "for the purpose," so he alleged, "of promoting the civilization and commerce of Africa, and for other humane and benevolent purposes." Leopold announced to the world that the Association had decided to remold the Congo "in harmony with modern ideas." Several European nationalities were represented in the Association, but it was significant that no Congolese were included.

The "philanthropic state" that Leopold proposed would be of inestimable benefit to all concerned. Among its other boons, it would assure that "the European merchant shall go hand in hand with the dark African trader; and justice, law and order shall prevail; and murder and lawlessness and the cruel barter of slaves shall forever cease."

Leopold's plans sounded honorable—indeed, highminded. In 1884, with the support of England, he persuaded other

KING LEOPOLD II OF BELGIUM   *Although he seemed to be a wise and benevolent ruler in most domestic matters, his policies in the Congo were nevertheless ruthless and indefensibly inhumane.*

European states to recognize him as king of the so-called "Congo Free State." In April, 1885, the Belgian parliament gave its stamp of approval to his claim to exclusive, personal rule over that "philanthropic" area. With that measure, Leopold became absolute ruler of a piece of real estate some 80 times larger than Belgium itself.

In 1888, the first of Leopold's official decrees struck the Congolese people. All vacant land, they woke up to discover, belonged to "the State," i.e., to Leopold. "Vacant land" was defined as all land not actually improved. The Congolese found themselves robbed of everything except their houses and their gardens. The vast forests in which they had hunted for countless generations and in which they had collected all the raw materials for their crafts, had now become, by fiat, Leopold's private preserves.

Edicts followed thick and fast. Africans were forbidden to trade in ivory, rubber, or any other natural product. A Congolese who gathered rubber, even for his own personal use, was to be treated as a poacher.

The white agents of the State-owned rubber monopoly were paid under a system that encouraged abuse; theoretically, at least, the less the African workers were paid for their labor, the more the overseers retained for themselves.

By 1900, forced labor was the norm. Africans were not permitted to move from their villages. They were made to pay enormous taxes in the form of rubber, ivory, and other local products. When they occasionally protested, their complaints were interpreted as revolt, and the natives were brutally crushed. Horrified observers spoke of "long miles of ruined, smoldering villages, thickly strewn with skeletons."

A Belgian merchant recorded this observation:

"There is not an inhabited village left in four days' steaming through a country formerly so rich; today, utterly ruined. The soldiers sent out to get rubber and ivory are depopulating the country. They find the quickest and cheapest method is to raid villages, seize prisoners, and have them redeemed afterwards for ivory."

Most of the hostages were women. The Africans, as do most primitive people, accounted their females as their wealth. Not only were the soldiers taking their wives and daughters from them, but in a very real sense, their capital was being appropriated. The rape of the nubile was common.

STATUE OF LEOPOLD   *This equestrian figure of the king was erected in the Congolese city once known as Leopoldville. Since the Democratic Republic of the Congo gained its independence from Belgium in 1960, black men have asserted their national pride by changing the old European names of their major cities into African names. Thus, in 1966, under President Joseph D. Mobutu, the capital city of Leopoldville was renamed Kinshasa. Similarly, Stanleyville became Kisangani, and Elisabethville is now called Lubumbashi.*

Still, for Leopold the rubber did not pile up fast enough. The king then conscripted thousands of Africans, and armed them with rifles. At gun point, Congolese workers were forced to increase their rubber output. Black troops were encouraged to commit atrocities upon their fellow countrymen, and were also told not to waste ammunition. Sadism proliferated beyond belief. Black soldiers cut off the right hands and the sexual organs of their victims, dried them, and brought them in baskets to their supervisors as evidence of their zeal in the service of the Great White King.

Excess piled upon excess, and horror upon horror. Africans accused of laziness were forced to drink white men's urine. Some European agents compelled their workers to actually eat the rubber if they deemed that the rubber had been badly prepared. Multitudes of Africans died from indigestion.

Leopold's overseers themselves were wretchedly paid. No matter how efficient they proved to be, they found themselves in debt a large part of the time. They, too, were caught up in a machine from which there was no escape, for Leopold did not intend that they should ever leave the Congo, or ever have the opportunity to disclose the brutality. If an agent tried to get away, he too, was hunted down like a criminal.

Stories of what was happening in the Congo gradually seeped out of the stricken country, like pus from a festering sore, and eventually became known in Europe. An underswell of hostile criticism arose. Some of Leopold's supporters dismissed the reports as "the vaporings of worthy souls whose reserves of sentimentalism are often injudiciously employed." But the critics were not so easily silenced. As the charges mounted, Leopold was hard put to convince his accusers, many of whom were missionaries, that he was not responsible for the atrocities. He even sent a Commission of Inquiry to the Congo, which consisted of a Belgian, a Swiss, and an Italian. The commission collected its evidence. The report was so horrifying that Leopold dared not have it published. Only the more innocuous parts of the document ever saw the light of day.

By now, the stench from the Congo reached all over the world. In 1903, the English sent a representative to Leopold's private fiefdom. His report denounced Leopold out of hand. A mounting tide of indignation crossed the Channel and rolled directly into Belgium, and soon the royal butcher was under pressure from his own government.

However, Leopold was adamant. He was not to be bullied as easily as were his advisers. As late as 1906, when Brussels was awash with the scandal, the contemptuous Leopold had the audacity to declare: "My rights on the Congo are indivisible. They are the result of my toil." This from a man who had never set foot in the land he arrogantly claimed to govern.

BRINGING IN RUBBER   *Under armed guard, Africans carry bales of rubber to the collecting station.*

AT THE COLLECTING STATION   *With their quotas of rubber on their heads, Africans—including children—line up for the
agent's inspection. White agent and black overseers stand together
at left of picture.*

Finally, the world's patience was exhausted. The British
proposed sending troops to the Congo to stop the atrocities,
and Brussels winced. The Belgian government defied Leopold and itself took over the administration of the Congo. It
was a unique picture; a loyal parliament taking a treasured
prerogative away from its otherwise quite popular king, a
king widely regarded in Europe as a wise monarch in his
own country.

Before he was stopped, Leopold had extracted a private profit of millions from the Congo rubber forests. He had also managed to murder some two-thirds of the Congolese people. Under his administration, the Congo's population had dropped from somewhere around 25 million to less than eight million. Some districts had lost 90 percent of their inhabitants. Whole towns had disappeared, stamped out by the boots of Leopold's overseers.

Even today, the memory of the "Royal Butcher" still poisons Africa's relations with the West.

PROCESSING RUBBER   *Over an open fire, Africans treat the*
raw latex they have collected.

THE PROFUMO SCANDAL

Perhaps the most sensational scandal of recent English history was that of John D. Profumo, the British Minister of War in 1963. It had everything: sex; espionage; the disgrace of a Cabinet Minister and member of the Queen's Privy Council; and finally a sensational trial followed by an equally sensational suicide.

Apart from Profumo, the important figures in the story are Stephen Ward, a talented and immoral osteopath; Eugene Ivanov, Russian Naval Attache and spy; and Christine Keeler, a showgirl of easy morals around whom the whole affair revolves in a kaleidoscope of whoredom, indiscretion and good old British hypocrisy.

It used to be said that the elements of a good newspaper story—sex, religion and class—were contained in the sentence: "My God, Bishop," said the Duchess, "take your hand off my knee." In the Profumo affair you can substitute espionage for religion. Certainly the aristocracy was well represented in the person of Viscount Astor, whose family has played a prominent part in British politics and who became a close friend of Stephen Ward's. Lord Astor succeeded his father in 1952 and inherited Cliveden, one of the more famous of Britain's stately homes. Following the tradition of his father, he entertained there many distinguished and respected social and political figures.

In 1950, while hunting, Lord Astor injured himself in a fall. He went to Stephen Ward for treatment and was so successfully cured that he referred many of his friends to him. Further, he lent Ward money, guaranteed his overdrafts, entertained him at Cliveden; and most important, in 1956, he rented a cottage to him on the Cliveden estate at a peppercorn rate. Here Ward entertained his girls. He had men friends, too, for perversion was also part of the entertainment offered in the Cliveden weekend cottage. Flagellation and the practice of homosexuality were among the less recondite pursuits.

Stephen Ward was fifty, son of a clergyman, a skilled osteopath, and an accomplished portrait painter. He was a man of great charm and ease of manner. Inevitably, his conversational gifts attracted some and repelled others. Some found him enormously likeable, others thought him merely a plausible fellow. A social climber and a name dropper, he loved the company of peers. He was also a great libertine and was often to be found in the company of prostitutes, both professional and amateur, pornographers, brothelkeepers, and individuals who organized flagellation parties.

He professed to be a communist and a passionate admirer of the Soviet Union. He made no secret of his political views, though his friends generally ignored them, for they regarded him as being slightly mad.

It is not unusual for those who indulge in sexual excess to become impotent. There is evidence that this was the case with Stephen Ward by the time the story of his peculiar activities burst upon a fascinated world. The sexual part of his story, as told at the Old Bailey, was disillusioning. The popular image of him was of a virile man of fifty enjoying legions of beautiful girls; whereas the truth, blurted out by one of his call-girl friends, was that he could no longer perform the sexual act and could only achieve satisfaction out of artificial vibro-massage. He had developed a preference for colored men and girls, and derived much of his sexual pleasure out of being whipped and used orally by his partners.

Ward was also a first-class bridge player, and he was one of the few people known to have introduced sex into this highly respectable game. When the company was right, the end of the penultimate rubber would be signaled by the appearance of a troop of girls, wearing little more than leather boots, who burst into the room brandishing whips and proceeded to treat the bridge players both to a fantastic cabaret and anything else that their peculiar fancies might desire.

Ward especially liked girls of sixteen and seventeen. He used to pick them up, usually at night clubs, and frequently had more than one of them living with him. It was remarked that he seduced many of them himself. However, in view of the doubt cast on his potency, as well as the improbable virginity of girls who regularly frequent London night clubs, it is more likely that what he did was to introduce them to those visceral fancies popular among his influential friends—particularly flagellation. For many of Ward's friends were graduates of those English private schools where flogging on the buttocks is still a punishment; an early initiation which often explains a future desire for flagellation.

One of the call girls of Ward's circle said, after the trial, that she never had had standard sex relations with any of her clients, many of whom were rich and influential. Flagellation was most commonly demanded by such clients. This act was sometimes performed by a girl wearing underclothes and high-heeled shoes or boots. After being whipped and trodden under her feet, the client would then, at the girl's command, perform cunnilingus upon her. This particular call girl reckoned that her list of client names and addresses was worth a small fortune.

At his trial, Stephen Ward was accused and found guilty of procuring. The verdict has been challenged, but there is no

IN HAPPIER DAYS   John Profumo appears with his wife and with R. A. Butler at a Conservative Party garden party—before he ever met Christine.

THE PROFUMOS IN 1959   John and Valerie canvass in Stratford-on-Avon, in the General Election campaign of 1959.

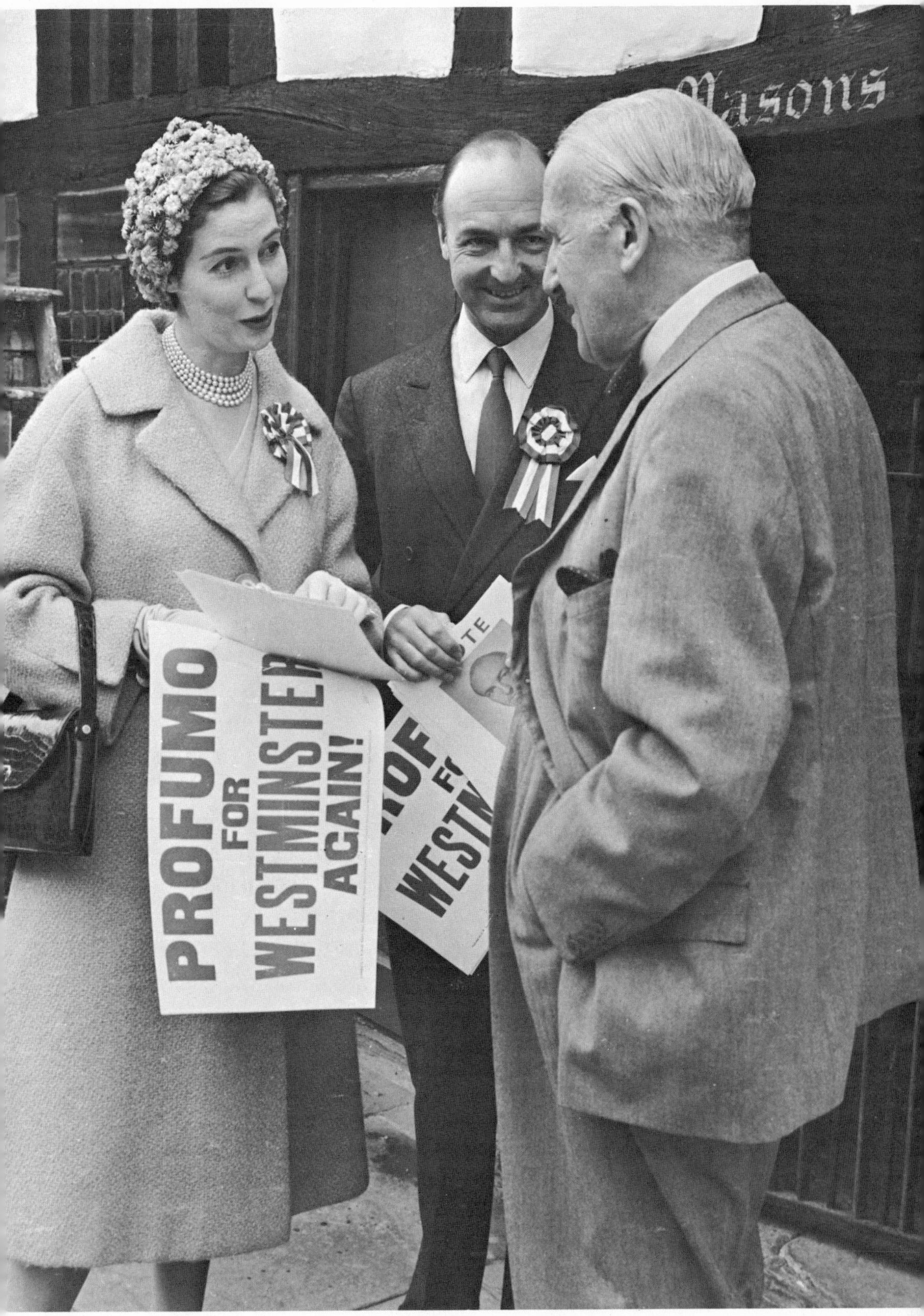
Masons
PROFUMO FOR WESTMINSTER AGAIN!

doubt that he did provide a number of his influential friends with girls. There was little evidence that money was paid out in these transactions. It was more likely that he was doing his friends a favor.

The most famous of the Ward girls was Christine Keeler, a petite, curiously attractive girl with red hair and a certain animal appeal, who was the center of the storm of hysteria which swept the British nation during the summer of 1963. She lived originally in Wraysbury on the River Thames. After being seduced by an American sergeant in her mid-teens, she went to find fame, if not fortune, in London. She got a job in the Murray Cabaret Club as a show girl, which involved, as she put it, just walking around with no clothes on.

She met Ward at Murray's and after a few meetings went to live with him at his London home, 17 Wimpole Mews. Throughout their association, it was said, they remained on Platonic terms. She came completely under his control; although she left him several times, she always came back.

Christine was just one of the flock of girls who was part of the Ward menage. He introduced them to his influential friends. There were always beds available at Wimpole Mews or the Cliveden cottage for the fun and games Ward's friends expected him to provide. There were orgies a-plenty, especially for those with a taste for being whipped by pretty girls.

Christine Keeler had many lovers, and among them was Captain Eugene Ivanov, the Assistant Naval Attaché at the Russian Embassy in London. British Secret Service was not long in discovering that Captain Ivanov was engaged in an important subsidiary activity—he was a member of Russian Intelligence and was actively spying in Britain. Ivanov was one of Ward's friends and shared many of Ward's tastes, including his passion for orgies. Ivanov has been described as "vulgar, jolly, sociable, a cheerful womanizer and good-natured." Ward's association with him had already come to

DR. STEPHEN WARD   A man of many hobbies—girls, whips, art, and espionage—the society osteopath relaxes at a friend's country home.

CAPTAIN EUGENE IVANOV Christine's Russian boyfriend is shown with his wife at an embassy reception in 1961. Christine once called him "a wonderfully huggy bear of a man." Formerly the assistant naval attache of the Soviet Embassy in London, he was recalled to Moscow in December, 1962, before the Profumo scandal came to light.

the attention of the British Secret Service, which in June, 1961, warned him that Ivanov was a spy and that any proposition he made to Ward should be passed on to them. Ward was delighted to find himself in touch with the Secret Service and promised to cooperate. He continued to be as friendly with Ivanov as before.

A month later came the two famous house parties. One took place at Cliveden where Lord Astor was entertaining a party of distinguished guests, including John Profumo and his wife, actress Valerie Hobson; the other was at Ward's cottage where the weekenders included Ivanov, Christine Keeler, and a mixed party of Ward's "special" friends.

There was a swimming pool at Cliveden which Lord Astor permitted Ward and his friends to use. On Saturday evening, July 8, Ward and some of his girls, Christine Keeler among them, were swimming in the pool. Christine somehow lost her swimsuit and was swimming in the nude when Lord Astor arrived at the poolside with some of his guests, among them Mr. and Mrs. Profumo. Christine hid her nakedness with a towel and the whole incident was treated as a piece of more or less innocent fun. The following day, there was a bathing party attended by Ward and his girls as well as Astor, War Minister Profumo, and Russian spy Ivanov. "Nothing indecent took place at all" during that party, to quote the words of Lord Denning in his report on the affair.

Profumo took a decided liking to Christine, and she was evidently flattered at being fancied by a person of such prominence. Ivanov, no doubt finding the situation highly promising from a Russian intelligence point of view, returned to town with Christine where they indulged in a session of alcoholic love-making at Ward's house. A great deal was made of this, in view of what immediately followed. Lord Denning says that Ivanov was never Christine's lover, even though "there were perhaps some kind of sexual relations" on that alcoholic Sunday night—a curious distinction on which his lordship sheds no further light.

But John Profumo certainly did become Christine's lover within the next few days and with Stephen Ward's active encouragement. Ward provided them with the proper, or perhaps improper, facilities at 17 Wimpole Mews. When his wife was away, Profumo took Christine to his house in Regent's Park. He also took to driving her around London in an official car with a ministerial mascot on it. He wrote her letters and gave her money and presents.

In the meantime, Ward had told the British Secret Service that Ivanov had asked him to find out just when the Americans were going to provide West Germany with nuclear weapons.

The alarm in the British Secret Service should have been acute. Here was the British Secretary of State for War not only friendly with a close friend of a Russian agent, but apparently sharing the agent's mistress as well. But, rather to the discredit of the British Secret Service, it knew nothing at the time of the War Minister's affair with Christine Keeler. It merely warned the Secretary of the Cabinet that Profumo should be careful in his dealings with Ward since any pearls of information he might drop would surely be passed on to Ivanov.

The warning was passed on to Profumo on August 9. It was a great shock to him, as he immediately imagined his affair with Christine Keeler had been discovered by the British Secret Service. He had a date with her the following night, and he realized that if he did not end the affair he would find himself in deep water indeed. He immediately wrote her this letter:

> *Darling—In great haste, because I can get no reply from your phone. Alas, something's blown up tomorrow night, and I can't therefore make it. I'm terribly sorry, as I leave the next day for various trips and then a holiday, so won't be able to see you again until sometime in September. Blast it. Please take great care of yourself and don't run*

CHRISTINE   Miss Keeler displays the form that rocked a government.

LORD ASTOR   The epitome of upper-class leisure, Lord Astor enjoys Gold Cup Day at Royal Ascot race track. Looking urbane and relaxed, he arrived with Lady Astor from their home, Cliveden, along with some 20 guests. It was a lucky day, as several of the party had placed bets on "Twilight Alley," winner of the Gold Cup at odds of 100 to 30. After the race, they toasted the jockey in champagne. Then they drove back to Cliveden for the usual Ascot party.

Lord Astor is shown here in the Owners' and Jockeys' Car Park at Ascot.

It was at Lord Astor's estate that John Profumo met Christine Keeler.

away—Love, J. P.S. I'm writing this 'cos I know you're off for the day tomorrow and I want you to know before you go if I still can't reach you by phone.

The whole business might well have ended there but for the subsequent activities of Christine Keeler and Stephen Ward. John Profumo had done nothing wrong, apart from committing the commonest of man's indiscretions. Many statesmen of the past have consorted with ladies of easy virtue without damage to their political careers.

What the authorities did not know was that Ward and Ivanov had tried to persuade Christine Keeler to get information from Profumo about America's intention to arm West Germany with nuclear weapons. Christine, who was no fool, flatly refused to have anything to do with such dangerous activities. She had no intention of playing Mata Hari. Profumo, as soon as he knew that she and Stephen Ward were on intimate terms with a Russian agent, dropped them like hot potatoes; although some reports say that he saw Christine several times afterwards and that their association lasted until December, 1961.

Ward, still fast friends with Ivanov, got in touch with the Foreign Office through Lord Astor, offering his services as an intermediary in the affair. He received an icy negative from the Foreign Office, which was under no illusions about him. He could not, however, be totally ignored in view of the fact that he knew so many influential people.

In October, 1962, Ward even attempted to intervene with Ivanov in the Cuban crisis. His delusions of grandeur were such that he believed he could be the instrument in getting Ivanov to act as intermediary between Washington and Moscow. The activities of the two men were greeted with increased suspicion. When Russian ships turned back from Cuba, Khrushchev's bluff having been called by President Kennedy, Ivanov could not conceal his anger and disappointment. The result was that Ward came under even stricter surveillance by the British Secret Service.

Meanwhile, Christine Keeler got herself involved in a sen-

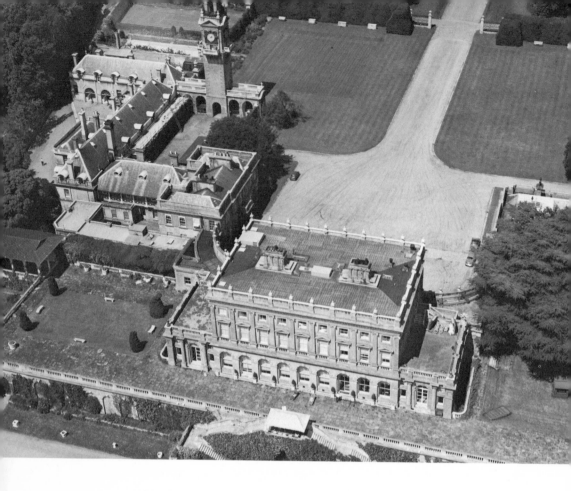

CLIVEDEN Amid house parties at Lord Astor's ·elegant country estate, Stephen Ward entertained his friends. Behind the tower at left is the swimming pool where Profumo met Christine.

sational affair with two West Indian gentlemen, "Lucky" Gordon and John Edgecombe, who fought over her in a night club. Consequently, Gordon went to hospital and required seventeen stitches to mend his slashed face. Christine then went to live with Edgecombe for a time but, tiring of him, she returned to Ward. Here she joined her friend Mandy Rice-Davies, another of Ward's girls, who had been the mistress of a slum property racketeer named Peter Rachman.

On December 14, 1962, Edgecombe came in search of Christine, determined to get her back, and raised riot with a gun outside 17 Wimpole Mews. This time he was arrested and charged not only with the shooting, but with slashing "Lucky" Gordon.

This incident brought Christine Keeler and Ward to the attention of the press—and Christine started to talk. Soon the story of her affair with Profumo became common knowledge, though the press was not yet able to publish it because of English libel laws.

All the same, the *Sunday Pictorial* bought her story for £1,000 and, after hearing what she had to say, the reporters on the *Pictorial* wrote her story for her:

> *Men are such fools. But I like them. I have always liked them.*
>
> *Unfortunately the combination of these things has led me into a lot of trouble and may even have risked the security of this country. It certainly could have been harmful to the country.*
>
> *You see, one man who was foolish enough and irresponsible enough to have an affair with me was a Cabinet Minister, a member of Her Majesty's Government.*
>
> *And at the same time I was having an affair with another man—a Russian diplomat.*

WARD'S COTTAGE On Lord Astor's estate at Cliveden, this Thames-side cottage was the site of varied hanky-panky.

If that Russian or anyone else had placed a tape recorder or cine camera or both in some hidden place in my bedroom it would have been very embarrassing for the Minister, to say the least.

In fact it would have left him open to the worst possible kind of blackmail—the blackmail of a spy.

I am not suggesting that he really would have given up State secrets to avoid a scandal. He might have been tough and refused.

But I do believe that any man in his position—particularly a married man—is both unwise and irresponsible to have an affair with some unknown girl like me.

More especially so in that case because this Minister has such knowledge of the military affairs of the Western world that he would be one of the most valuable men in the world for the Russians to have had in their power.

He is in fact the Secretary of State for War, Mr. John Profumo.

I believe now that a man in his position should not indulge in pastimes like me. I suppose even Cabinet Ministers are only human, but I think they should curb their feelings when they take on the job.

One might think that as a politician he would have been particularly discreet in the affair. John Profumo was not. It is true he did not take me out much, but he did take me to his own home while his wife was away. And he did write letters to me.

One might also think that those responsible for State security would keep some sort of watch on men who hold as many secrets as he holds.

Yet if it happened he would never have been able to come and see me at the flat where I was being visited by the Russian.

And, believe me, the Russian was a man who would be very much aware of the value of the secrets which Profumo knew. He was not a civilian.

He was in fact a naval captain, Captain Eugene Ivanov.

Of course at the time I did not realize the sinister implications behind my two affairs. I was only

18 and knew nothing of politics or international matters. I was not interested.

I did not realize then that blackmail is one of the Russians' favourite weapons when they are trying to recruit traitors or discover secret information.

I am sure that Jack Profumo would not have allowed his harmless affair with me to be used as a lever to prise secrets from him. But a weaker man in his position might have allowed it to happen.

At the time, however, I saw no danger in the situation. It just seemed funny to me that I should be seeing the two men, sometimes on the same day. One might leave my flat only a few minutes before the other arrived.

I did find it worrying when someone asked me to try to get from Profumo the answer to a certain question.

That question was: "When, if ever, are the Americans going to give nuclear weapons to Germany?"

I am not prepared to say in public who asked me to find out the answer to that question. I am prepared to give it to the security officials. In fact, I believe now that I have a duty to do so.

There is a certain piquancy about the year's most notorious call girl lecturing British Security in particular and cabinet ministers in general on their duties. It is also interesting to reflect that while she was prepared to name Profumo and thus ruin him, she was not prepared to name Ward publicly. Ward, in view of his open dabbling in espionage, had far less to lose than Profumo.

The existence of this story, which had been signed and au-

TOWN HOUSE   Ward's London home was the scene of numerous orgies and assignations, including Christine's sex-and-booze evening with Ivanov, and several of her meetings with Profumo. The prosecutor's charge against Ward alleged that "He, being a man, on diverse dates between January 1, 1961, and June 8, 1963, knowingly lived wholly or in part on the earnings of prostitution at 17 Wimpole Mews, London, W.L."

thorized page by page by Christine Keeler, caused a furor.
The strongest possible pressure was put on the newspaper to
prevent publication. Ward and Lord Astor were in constant
session with their attorneys. When John Profumo heard that
Christine Keeler had told her story to the *Sunday Pictorial* he
was, not unnaturally, in a state of great alarm; and his attorneys became frantically busy in an attempt to suppress the
appalling revelations Christine proposed to make. Among the
choice pieces of evidence she had given to the newspaper to
back up her story was the "Darling" letter Profumo had
written to her on August 9, 1961.

Christine, through her attorneys, said she wanted £5000
to kill the story. She said later that she should have asked for
£50,000. The *Sunday Pictorial* finally decided that it was not
safe to publish her story, and all she got out of it was £200
advance on the £1000 they had agreed to pay on publication.

On August 28, 1963, the Attorney-General saw Profumo
and told him that he was the subject of serious rumors dissem-
inated by a young girl, and that if there were any truth to these
rumors he would have to resign. Profumo denied the truth of
Christine Keeler's story, and was then told that he would have
to institute proceedings if such a story were published. Other
government officials, concerned for the good name of the
Queen's ministers, also saw the Minister for War, who again
stoutly denied that there was anything improper in his association with Christine Keeler. He denied that he had slept with
her, and said he was merely waiting for an opportunity to take
action to refute the story.

The opportunity came when a private newsletter called *The
Westminister Confidential,* a stenciled sheet distributed to
about two hundred subscribers, referred to the fact that certain call girls had begun to sell their stories to the Sunday
newspapers. It added:

> *One of the choice bits in their story was a letter*

*LUCKY GORDON AT HOME   In his London flat, Jamaican night club sing-
er Aloysius "Lucky" Gordon relaxes after the court hearing in which Christine
Keeler was accused of plotting and lying to send him to prison.*

*Gordon smiled once during the five-minute hearing when the Magistrate said
Christine could be released on bail. With Paula Hamilton-Marshall and Mrs.
Olive Brooker, her housekeeper, Christine was accused of perjuring herself at
Gordon's earlier trial at the Old Bailey. At the trial, Lucky was sentenced to
three years for assaulting Christine. The sentence was later quashed by the
Court of Criminal Appeal.*

CHRISTINE KEELER *Looking disheveled, Christine arrives at her London apartment. She had been at a secret hideout on the South Coast but had rushed home when she heard on her car radio that her former boyfriend, Lucky Gordon, had been freed from prison. "I'm frightened," she said. "I am going into my flat and locking the door. I shall not move unless I get police protection." Gordon had previously been convicted of assaulting Christine but he had appealed and was now acquitted.*

apparently signed on the stationery of the Secretary for War. The allegation by this girl was that not only was this minister, who has a famous actress for his wife, her client, but also the Soviet Military Attache, apparently a Colonel Ivanov. The famous actress wife, of course, would sue for divorce, the scandal ran. Who was using the call girl to milk whom of information—the War Secretary or the Soviet Military Attache—ran the minds of those primarily interested in security.

There was no question that this paragraph defames John Profumo. However, no action was taken against *The Westminister Confidential*. Its circulation was too limited. Both the Attorney-General and Profumo's legal advisers agreed that action here was wasteful and inadvisable.

The trial of John Edgecombe was fast approaching; a trial at which Christine Keeler would be a key witness. It was expected that she would tell the story of her relationship with Profumo and Ivanov in the witness box. In fact, she disappeared at the last minute. She went off to Spain with two friends, Paul Mann and Kim Procter. Later she said she went because she was scared of what she was getting herself into; and also because she had heard that two colored men were to be paid to "cut her up."

The newspapers, naturally enough, pursued her, making increasingly attractive bids for her story.

MAN OF MANY ARTS With girlfriend Julie Gulliver, Dr. Stephen
Ward arrives at a Museum Street art gallery to view an exhibition of
his drawings. His happy, casual expression was soon to turn into
suicidal despair.

The trial was therefore held without the key witness, to the accompaniment of rumors that Christine had been spirited away for political reasons. Edgecombe got seven years for possessing a firearm with intent to endanger life but was acquitted on the shooting charges.

Lord Denning, in his investigation of the scandal, found no evidence of any intent on the part of Profumo or Astor to obstruct the course of justice by causing Christine Keeler to disappear. The Lord Chief Justice at the Court of Criminal Appeal remarked: "The fact that the jury acquitted on the first two [shooting] charges seems to this court natural in the absence of the girl."

Denning, in his report, commented on the widespread suspicion that Christine Keeler's disappearance was maneuvered for political reasons. "It was thought to be in Mr. Profumo's interest that she should disappear and he was supposed to be at the back of it," he said.

On March 14, the widely circulated *Daily Express* ran a front page story under the banner line: WAR MINISTER SHOCK. It stated that Profumo had offered his resignation "for personal reasons," but that Prime Minister Harold Macmillan had asked him to stay on. On the same page there was a picture of Christine Keeler headed VANISHED OLD BAILEY WITNESS. In view of the English laws of libel and contempt of court, newspapers always take a risk in placing such closely related stories in juxtaposition. The *Daily Express* was criticized on the grounds that the two stories taken togehter might be defamatory in the minds of those readers who had heard the rumors.

Members of the Cabinet were gravely concerned, but the law officers of the government said there was no case for action. The *Express* had a good case for saying that the juxtaposition of the two stories was entirely coincidental. Indeed many people think that English law is too sensitive on these

AT THE ART SHOW While facing trial on seven vice charges, Ste-
phen Ward took time out to open an astonishing moneymaking exhibition
of his drawings. In normally quiet Museum Street in Bloomsbury, crowds
thronged the little London art Gallery where Ward put up 144 sketches
for sale. Here, amid TV arc lamps, popping flashbulbs, stares, and cheers,
Mandy Rice-Davies drinks a toast: "Here's to Stephen! Good old Ste-
phen!"

Mandy, the "great friend" of Ward, was not known for her reticence.
She appeared to be demure and childlike, and the press found her dis-
armingly frank, ready to call a spade a spade. She described herself as
"a modern Lady Hamilton," and was for many months a national figure.

matters.

Things had reached such a pass by now that the government considered it necessary for John Profumo to make a personal statement in the House of Commons, where the matter
had already been raised by George Wigg, the Labour Member
for Dudley.

Profumo still refused to admit the truth of his relationship with Christine Keeler. His fellow members of the Cabinet considered him an honorable man who would not lie about such a matter. Therefore a statement was drafted by the Attorney-General and Solicitor-General which Profumo read in the House of Commons on March 22, 1963. It said that he had only a slight acquaintance with Christine Keeler and that there was no impropriety whatsoever in his relationship with her. He denied he had any hand in her disappearance at the time of the Edgecombe trial. And, he added, if anyone said otherwise, he would not hesitate to issue writs for libel and slander.

"He's a liar," said a Conservative Member when Profumo made the statement, and many people who knew the facts were of the same opinion.

What made Profumo think he could get away with it was one of the mysteries of the whole curious affair. His ex-mistress supported him up to a point. In the *News of the World* (March 31, 1963) she reneged on the unpublished story she had given to the *Sunday Pictorial* and declared: "Certainly, both he and his wife were friends of mine. But it was a friendship no one can criticize." She was paid £100 for the story.

Profumo doubtless thought that his sole guilt lay in the fact that he had committed adultery with the girl. So far as he was concerned the security of the country was never at any time in jeopardy through his association with her; and his conscience was clear about her disappearance at the time of the Edgecombe trial. Why throw away his whole political career on account of a brief affair with a call girl?

But once having told the big lie in the House of Commons, there was no turning back. When two foreign magazines overstepped the bounds of what was permitted under the English libel law, Profumo successfully sued both of them.

These prosecutions angered many people who were in possession of the true facts, and the affair was not allowed to rest. Later, Profumo had to pay heavy damages to the two magazines because of his unwarranted claim against them.

The Home Office now began to investigate the activities of Stephen Ward, particularly his relationship with Ivanov; and Ivanov's relationship with Christine Keeler. Ivanov had hurriedly left the country. The British Secret Service, which operates under the direction of the Home Office, now came into the possession of Christine's statement that Ward had urged her to ask Profumo for information about America's intention to provide West Germany with nuclear weapons. Concurrently police were investigating Ward's activities with his girls and the allegation that he was living on their earnings.

Ward then sought an interview with the Prime Minister's Private Secretary and told him that if the police did not stop their inquiries into his activities, he would expose Profumo's sexual relations with Christine Keeler. He said he had done much to shield Profumo from his indiscretion, and the least the authorities could do was to leave him alone.

This was the end for Profumo. Ward wrote to Harold Wilson, then Leader of the Opposition: "Obviously my efforts to conceal the fact that Mr. Profumo had not told the truth in Parliament have made it look as if I myself had something to hide. It is quite clear now that they must wish the facts to be known, and I shall see that they are." He sent copies of this letter to the newspapers. More questions were asked in Parliament; the British Secret Service was nosing into the affair; and the Lord Chancellor was holding an inquiry.

The pressure on Profumo became intolerable. At the beginning of June, 1963, he and his wife went to Venice for a short holiday, relentlessly pursued by the press. Profumo, who now felt like a hunted man, decided he could no longer hide behind his untruths. Too many people knew he had lied to the House. It was just a matter of time before he would be forced

SURPRISE WITNESS   Amid the varied gazes of onlookers, elegantly dressed Ronna Ricardo, 23-year-old ex-dancer from a Paris night club, moves toward Marylebone Magistrates Court to be called as a prosecution witness in the Stephen Ward vice trial. She was notified only ten hours before the trial opened that she was wanted as a witness.

MANDY AND THE COPS Perfectly cool and calm, 18-year-old *Marilyn Rice-Davies leaves court. After spending a brief holiday in Majorca, Mandy had returned to England to be interviewed by Lord Denning in his investigation of security aspects of the Profumo affair.*

to admit it.

He confessed the whole business to his wife, who was apparently very understanding. She said, "Darling, we must go home now, just as soon as we can, and face up to it."

They returned the next day, and on June 4, he told the Prime Minister's Private Secretary that he had lied to the

EAGER CROWDS   As Dr. Stephen Ward leaves court during his vice trial, cordons of bobbies hold back the crowds. Throughout the hearings, people thronged the court and its vicinity, hoping to catch glimpses of the central figures in this juiciest of scandals.

BRAVING THE RAIN   Dauntless crowds line up for the first sessions of Stephen Ward's vice trial. First witness for the prosecution was red-haired Christine Keeler whom Ward had introduced to War Minister John Profumo, and whose revelations nearly toppled the government of Prime Minister Harold Macmillan. Prosecutor Mervyn Griffith-Jones accused Ward of having sexual intercourse with girls under 21, running a "brothel" of models for his male friends, aiding in abortion, and living off the girls' earnings in a luxurious apartment equipped with a "see-through" bedroom mirror.

House and that his relationship with Christine Keeler had been sexual. He then handed in his resignation to the Prime Minister, both as a Minister and as a Member of Parliament. He sent his seals of office, by messenger, to the Queen. His name was removed from the Privy Council. His disgrace was complete.

Meanwhile, Christine Keeler sold her story to the *News of*

the World for £23,000, and the Sunday after Profumo's resignation the first installment appeared. On June 21, Lord Denning was asked to make a full inquiry into the circumstances of the scandal.

Even though British Security had been informed that the War Minister had shared a mistress with a notorious Russian agent and that the girl had been asked to find out certain

important military information, the security aspect of the affair was not taken seriously by the authorities until Denning emphasized it in his report.

After Profumo's resignation and disgrace, the authorities turned savagely on Stephen Ward, hounding him on the subject of his immorality and his comparatively unimportant offense of living in part on the sexual earnings of his girls. His trial was held between July 22 and 30, in an atomosphere of prudish hysteria and endless innuendoes. The prosecution's witnesses consisted mainly of a procession of prostitutes and call girls, a number of whom confessed afterwards that their evidence was perjured and that they had been put under intolerable pressure by the police to give evidence required by the prosecution. Moreover, they were too frightened to make public allegations against the police.

In June, "Lucky" Gordon was sentenced to three years' imprisonment for assaulting Christine Keeler. He appealed, and on July 30, while the Ward case was still in progress, the Court of Criminal Appeal quashed the sentence in circumstances which gave rise to the popular belief that Christine Keeler had given perjured evidence.

On the same day, the judge in the Ward trial began his summing up. He had not finished it when the court was adjourned. That night Ward took an overdose of drugs and in the morning was found unconscious. He left notes which indicated that he believed all was lost after the judge's floral

FIRST IN LINE   Spectators await entrance to the Public Gallery in Old Bailey to hear Stephen Ward's vice trial. Queues formed hours before the opening of the court.

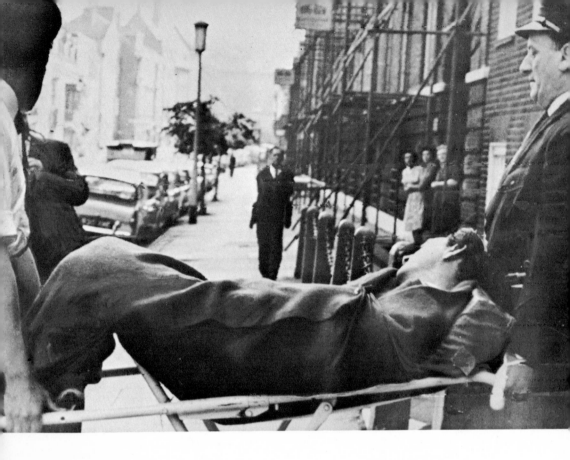

SUICIDE   Unconscious from an overdose of drugs, Dr. Stephen Ward is carried by attendants to an ambulance. Shortly before a criminal court jury was to begin deliberating on vice charges against him, Ward was found in his apartment. He never reganied consciousness, and died on August 3, 1963.

statement. Doubtless he was truly in despair. Lord Astor and all his other rich and influential friends, to whose sex life he had catered, had abandoned him and left him to face his fate alone.

The Court assembled at the Old Bailey the next morning, embarrassed and a little humiliated. There was barely any chance of Ward being resuscitated and brought before them again. The judge, looking a trifle sour, decided to continue the trial up to the point when the verdict was given by the jury, and this was done. Ward was found guilty of living on the immoral earnings of Christine Keeler and Mandy Rice-Davies. Sentence was postponed until Ward was fit to appear.

Ward, however, lay unconscious through all the histrionics which surrounded the end of the trial. He died on August 3, 1963. A wave of sympathy now mounted in his favor. The police, the authorities, the prosecutors at his trial were vilified. It was widely believed he had been convicted on perjured evidence and the unfortunate girls who had gone into the witness box for the Crown had been terrorized by the police into giving false testimony.

One call girl, in particular, after having told the police that she had whipped Stephen Ward at his flat, said that the police then suggested to her that she should also say that she had whipped other men there too. When she refused to give false evidence, the police threatened to prosecute her. She then made the depositions demanded of her. But she was too scared to repeat her story publicly even after the trial.

Although it was generally felt that Ward was convicted on perjured evidence, no one doubted that he had led an excessively immoral life and that he had procured girls for a number of distinguished men. He was not however charged with procurement. The names of the distinguished men, with the exception of Profumo who was finished anyway, were carefully kept out of the trial, and not one of them came to the Old

Bailey to speak a word in Ward's defense.

The trial itself showed Britain in one of its ugliest and most hypocritical moods. Witnesses like Christine Keeler had to run the gauntlet of leering and jeering crowds. Clergy, writers and politicians, pontificated sanctimoniously about the supposed collapse in national morals. However, reporters who attended the trial decided they had seen a miscarriage of justice.

Lord Denning issued his report in September, 1963. It was written in a somewhat racy style, obviously intended for mass consumption. It went into the scandal in detail. It dealt generously with the distinguished people involved (including Profumo), and ungenerously with the nonentities, particularly Ward, who now safely in his grave, received an over-full measure of contempt.

No comment was made on the fact that Ward's important and influential friends were in the market for young girls. Denning, on the other hand, went to some lengths to establish that other ministers of the Crown and people prominent in public life had not taken part in fancy sex parties, as was rumored at the time.

LUCKY AND HIS BRIDE   *Aloysius Gordon, 34-year-old jazz singer, is shown with his bride of a few days, the former Helen Shepherd, 21. The two had met about a year earlier when she had asked a friend to introduce her to him.*

Helen's father, Alexander Shepherd of Stonehaven, Scotland, caught a train to London on the morning of the wedding, hoping to stop his daughter from marrying Gordon. But father and daughter did not meet, and Helen spoke to him only on the telephone. Said Helen later "We waited for my 21st birthday before making the final arrangements for the wedding. I wrote and told my parents then. . . . I knew they would never consent to me marrying Lucky. They are terribly prejudiced because of what they have read of him about the Christine Keeler business. They have never met him."

Helen said that her mother, Mrs. Mary Shepherd, telephoned her and told her to tear up all the letters she had ever written. "She told me that I am no longer her daughter," said Helen.

Lucky commented: "I am willing to meet Helen's parents, because I have married their daughter and I love her. But from what she tells me, they are not likely to make it up." The jazz singer was out of work at the moment. "I have a few jobs coming up soon," he said.

MANDY WEDS Three years after the Profumo scandal, a shy and respectable Mandy Rice-Davies marries 26-year-old airline steward Rafael Shaul, the son of a wealthy Israeli merchant. Before the ceremony, the couple dodged reporters by entering the St. Marylebone Registry office by a back door. Only with difficulty were they persuaded to pose for this photograph. Mandy wore a green and oatmeal-colored costume, mauve stockings, and oatmeal-colored shoes; her blonde hair was tied at the back with a black bow. She had been singing in cabarets around the world, and met her husband in an Israeli cafe.

Lord Denning assured Britain that nothing was wrong with the country's security, even though he criticized the British Secret Service for not pursuing this aspect of the affair with sufficient zeal. He was right, however, in saying that there was no danger. John Profumo was a loyal subject with whom Her Majesty's secrets were perfectly safe. So, for that matter, was Christine Keeler, who had firmly refused to pump any secrets out of him. Stephen Ward's loyalties were certainly in doubt, as his traducers' standards were not of the highest. One of the officials who assisted Lord Denning in his inquiry said afterwards: "Well, I dare say we were a bit unfair to Ward. We were under a lot of pressure, as I expect you know, and we did not really have time to read the report of the trial in detail."

It was, of course, scandalous that Profumo should have lied to the House of Commons, though many have done so before him. Indeed, the lies told to the House at the time of the Suez affair in 1956 were far more damaging to the country than anything Profumo said or did. No one can dispute that Stephen Ward led a scandalous life, yet the men in prominent places, with the exception of Profumo, who urged him to procure girls for them got away with it completely.

The police, who had to interview no less than 140 witnesses before they could bring any kind of evidence against Ward, were never subjected to any public criticism; two of their star witnesses said afterwards that they lied in the witness box under police pressure, but were so terrified that they dared not admit it publicly. The whole unsavory affair ended on a shocking admission, by one of Lord Denning's officials, that the report had been unfair to Ward.

No one talks much about the Profumo scandal in England these days. Publishers are semiofficially discouraged from dealing with it.

The two chief participants in the affair dropped from the

BEST SELLING REPORT   Soon after midnight on the day of its release, crowds in Kingsway jostle to buy copies of the Denning report.

DISAPPROVING COLLEAGUE Minister of Health Enoch Powell walks out of Admiralty House after the second Cabinet meeting on the Profumo affair. Mr. Powell was reported to be the Minister who voiced strongest disapproval of the situation; there were rumors that he had threatened to resign.

MRS. PROFUMO   Valerie Hobson, the woman who stood by her husband throughout the entire scandal, buries her head in her hands and weeps.

public eye. Profumo took up social work at Toynbee Hall in London's East End. In February, 1968, he was appointed to the board of visitors at Grendon Psychiatric Prison, Buckinghamshire, a voluntary and unpaid job.

Christine Keeler married engineer James Levermore in October, 1965. The marriage broke up in January the following year, although Christine was expecting a baby. "I'm sure Jim

didn't marry me for my money," she said. "We just did not see
eye to eye on certain basic things."

As for Mandy Rice-Davies, the other girl whose immoral
earnings Ward lived from, she married an Israeli airline
steward, Rafael Shaul, in 1966, and now lives in Israel where
she runs a successful night club called "Mandy's."

*THE PROFUMO FAMILY Home after a holiday in the re-
mote north of Scotland comes John Profumo who had resigned
as War Minister a few months earlier. With him at London's
Euston Station are his wife, former actress Valerie Hobson, and
their son David, eight.*

THE GREAT SOUTH SEA BUBBLE

When the South Sea Company opened for business in 1711, it did so in the heart of one of the world's richest and most powerful cities—London. It did so at a time when London was not only the most populous city in Europe, but virtually a republic in itself—complete with its own army, and a Lord Mayor as powerful as any duke of the realm.

The new city, built upon the ashes of the Great Fire of 1666, was to 18th-century eyes almost unbelievable. The pinched, refuse-lined streets seemed wide thoroughfares to them, and narrow though they were, they bore more commerce per square foot than any other streets in Europe. Thronged with sedan chairs, with gilded coaches rolling on brightly colored wheels, London seemed elegant. Yet the rich lived cheek by jowl with indescribable poverty. Furs and silks and costly brocades brushed by the deformed bodies of beggars and the bloated stomachs of starving children.

The Thames was alive with shipping. Great counting houses flanked the city's streets. Merchants traded their stocks and shares in the offices of their day—the coffee houses of the city. Burgeoning prosperity and a boisterous optimism proclaimed themselves everywhere. This was a city and a country ripe for the fleecing. Speculation was in the air—and it was irresistible.

The Londoners' outlook was naive in the extreme. The early 18th-century Englishman thought the world outside his island a strange and mysterious place. His credulity was un-bounded; and his concept of economic reality was as severely limited as his knowledge of geography.

The optimism of London's speculators was not, however, entirely ungrounded, for it was based upon a solid and rapidly expanding economy. It was only when the Londoner turned his eyes beyond the seas—to the fancied riches of El Dorado —that he allowed unscrupulous men to perpetrate upon him one of the biggest swindles in history, a swindle followed by an economic crash of gigantic proportions.

With the Treaty of Utrecht, which terminated the War of the Spanish Succession, Britain exacted from Spain the right to trade with the Spanish Colonies. The Englishman imagined that untold riches were to be derived from this trade, and it was in this fancy that the great South Sea Bubble took shape.

It wasn't that the South Sea Company had anything specific to sell the public. In fact, the reverse was true. Its prospectus, to use a modern term, was pathetically vague. What was proffered was a powerful potion laced with legend and rumors of gold—a promise that put early 18th-century hands into pockets. Pounds from every conceivable source found their way into the coffers of the South Sea Company.

When the company was pressed to define just what it was selling, it presented a mishmash of half-truths and fantasy, and the South Sea Company had little trouble in selling its intangible wares. For the South Seas and South America were to the 18th-century Englishman as remote as the moun-tains of the moon. The term "South Seas" conjured up an area just off the western coasts of South America; the term had nothing at all to do with that part of the globe located in Polynesia. In the South Seas of the Englishman's misconcep-tion there were fabulous lands where gold was lying upon the ground waiting to be picked up, and where natives would exchange marvelous artifacts for a pittance. All the incredible wealth of this incredible land was to be had if only an efficient organization was put into being to exploit the riches.

Of course, there was little or no basis for these fantastic visions. Moreover, in pursuing this imaginary wealth, the South Sea Company was blithely ignoring the fact that very real and substantial profits could be made in exploiting the very real and substantial resources of South America. Had the promoters of the South Sea Company not been so intent on fleecing their countrymen, they might very well have found themselves genuinely wealthy, by being fully engaged in a hardheaded profitable business.

As it turned out, even as con men, the promoters were inept, for they ended up believing their own fantasies. The people of England were to suffer as much for the South Sea Company's self-delusion as for its dishonesty.

Money to exploit the South Sea dream poured into the offices and soon the company was backed by, or in league with, a reputable sword-making firm, the Sword Blade Company, which had recently turned itself into a finance house. From then on, the South Sea Company and Sword Blade Company worked hand in hand with interchangeable directors, and their fortunes rode from strength to strength on the crest of a national wave of speculation. The directors themselves were amazed at the success of their promotion. They had discovered, perhaps too early in history, the enormous power of advertising. They were in the business of concretizing a dream. In a society where the written word had a peculiar power and where there were still no laws to stop anyone from using the medium in any way he pleased, it didn't matter that the dream was unrealizable.

Huge quantities of South Sea stock were bought by an enthusiastic public. Reason was cast to the winds. Within weeks, gullibility was a contagion that was out of control.

There were a few who were immune. When Sir Isaac New-

FOLLY OF SPECULATION A contemporary cartoon illustrates the far-fetched

...recarious, destructive nature of the investment fever.

JAMES CRAGG THE ELDER   *Like many other high-ranking government officials, the Postmaster General made huge profits from his dealings with the South Sea Company. Afterward, on the day that the Parliamentary Committee of Inquiry made its report to the House, Cragg took poison. His son, James Cragg, Jr., who had also been seriously implicated in the swindle, died of smallpox on the same day.*

ton was asked his opinion of the South Sea stock, he replied that he could calculate the motion of the planets but not the madness of the people.

Real madness is certainly what it was. And it was not confined to the uneducated nor to the newly-rich mercantile classes. Great lords and princes, with superb credulity, invested thousands of pounds at a stroke. Within a matter of months, the capital of the South Sea Company rivaled that of the Bank of England.

In 1715, the Prince of Wales (later George II) was named as governor of the company. His motives, poor as they were, were probably no more ill-advised than those which spurred most of the other investors. The prince, anxious to become independent of his hated father, George I, needed lots of money of his own. But if the South Sea Company looked like the answer to his dreams, he was soon disabused of the notion, for he had reckoned without the king's own greed. When George I withdrew from his son all his princely privileges, the South Sea Company fawningly requested that the king himself become a governor of the company. George I, who figured he knew a good thing when he saw one, graciously agreed. He promptly invested £60,000—a huge sum in those days—in South Sea stock. He had been privately assured of enormous profits.

By this time, South Sea stock had been steadily inflating in value over a period of years, and the company's directors had long since become firmly convinced of the substantiality of the South Sea dream. So thorough was their self-delusion that in 1719, they proposed a scheme whereby the South Sea Company would take over the entire national debt, a matter of some £51,300,000. The debt consisted mainly of unredeemable state annuities, incurred during the wars against Louis XIV. Not only did the directors offer to take over the obligations of the British government, but they offered £3,-

500,000 for the privilege. Their plan, like all great quick-profit schemes, was based upon their certainty that all people want to get something for nothing. The directors proposed that the holders of state annuities exchange their long-term certificates for South Sea stock. The stock would be offered at a high premium, a price which would enable the South Sea Company to buy up a large number of annuities for a comparatively small amount of stock. A holder of a £100 annuity which was guaranteed for 80 years would be insane not to exchange it for South Sea stock worth £1,800 at par and paying a yearly dividend of £90. The dividend would, of course, increase as the company prospered.

When the bill to sanction the absorption of the national debt was presented to Parliament, the South Sea Company, in order to counter the opposition of the Bank of England, increased its bid to £7,500,000. This added incentive was hardly necessary, for anyone of importance had already been heavily bribed.

TRADING FRENZY   During the height of speculation in South Sea shares, investors and pickpockets are equally active.

The innermost leaders of His Majesty's Government from the Prime Minister, the Earl of Sunderland, down to the Postmaster General, James Cragg, stood to make—and did make—huge personal fortunes out of their connections with the company. The corruption extended to the Prince of Wales, and even to the king himself. It was complete.

The bill was railroaded through Parliament over the opposition of many of its more stalwart members. The stock spiraled upward. Then it soared. The boom was on, and it couldn't be checked.

A fever of speculation gripped England. The entire population was infected. Everyone invested, rich and poor alike— the aristocracy, the clerks, the clergy, army officers, ladies of fashion, ladies of easy virtue, including mistresses of both the king and the Prince of Wales. Half of continental Europe too, was gambling in South Sea stock. A delirious public subscribed vast sums, of which nearly 10 million pounds were spent in bribing politicians and market operators. In a few weeks, the company had persuaded over half the holders of Government annuities to become stockholders.

In 1719, when the South Sea scheme passed Parliament, the stock stood at £335. In June of 1720, it was quoted at £890. In July, the price had soared to £1,000 a share.

The South Sea Company's enormous success spawned any number of imitators. Companies were floated for truly remarkable projects: fishing for wrecks of the Spanish Armada off the Irish Coast, making oil from sunflower seeds, extracting silver from lead, transmuting quicksilver into metal. One company was dedicated to importing jackasses from Spain. The crowning glory was the setting up of a company for an undertaking "which shall in due time be revealed."

When the end came, it came abruptly and without warning. The South Sea Company, believing itself threatened by its imitators, tried to stop them by law. When it advised the

GEORGE, PRINCE OF WALES   *As governor of the South Sea Company,*
the heir to the throne hoped to become financially independent of his father.
But when his father took action, young George was deprived of both his
governorship and his princely privileges.

Whale Fishery

Whale Fishing, which was once a gainfull Trade,
Is now by cunning Heads, a Bubble made ;——
For round the Change they only spread their Sailes,
And to catch Gudgeons, bait their Hooks with Whale

OTHER RACKETS *In a pack of satirical eighteenth-century play-ing cards, each card debunks a different investment enterprise. Among the "bubbles" offered to the gullible public were companies specializing in whale fishing (left) and fire insurance (right). Other cards, not*

Rose Insurance from Fire

Projecting sure must be a Gainfull Trade,
Since all the Elements are Bubbles made,
They're right that gull us with ÿ Dread of Fire,
For fear makes Greater Fools, than Fond Desire.

shown, featured companies for bleaching hair, curing the "grand pox or clap," knitting stockings, "providing for and employing all the poor in Great Britain," and settling North American lands reportedly infested with lions and man-eating fish.

"CHANGE ALLEY" As would-be investors pawn their gems for ready cash, makeshift tables handle the overflow crowds.

GEORGE I The King of England, along with his son, his mistresses, and thousands of his countrymen, invested huge sums in the South Sea bubble. And even the King lost money when the bubble burst.

people of England—and rightly so—to distrust these unsound enterprises, the company found itself hoisted on its own petard. Prick one bubble, and you prick them all. Distrust one company, and you may well look askance upon all others.

The collapse came in September, 1720. People began to unload their stock. By the end of the month, South Sea stock, quoted at £1,000 in July, had dropped to £180.

Bankruptcy and despair gripped England from one end to the other. Thousands of people were ruined. Many, unable to meet their debts, fled the country. George I's investment of £60,000 shrank to £10,000, and he gloomily hurried home from Hanover.

By November, Britain's economic system was tottering. Credit dried up. Paper money was almost worthless. Banks closed, and prices collapsed. Unemployment rose. There were food riots. The South Sea Bubble had burst.

England's crash made Holland and France reel. To add to the general misery, a smallpox epidemic swept across Europe. In Marseilles, some 30,000 people died, and as the epidemic moved inexorably northwards, people saw in it the judgment of God upon fools.

That winter in England was bleak. Credit was frozen; trade, at a standstill. Beef was a penny a pound—payable by barter or in hard coin, no other exchange being acceptable.

The company reaped what it had sown. As ecstatic as the British had been in prosperity, so now were they furious in their despair. No one who had helped dupe the investor was spared a vengeful tongue, not even the king or his ministers.

But there was one major politician who, while the bubble expanded, had refused to feather his nest. Now the country turned as a man to Sir Robert Walpole. Over the anguished resistance of guilty ministers and tainted politicians, the House of Commons voted an official enquiry. The South Sea Company and the Sword Blade Bank frantically set themselves to altering their books and burning their accounts.

On January 24, 1720, five South Sea directors were arrested and brought before the House of Lords, where in due time, they finally admitted that huge sums had been paid as bribes to those ministers who helped in the passage of the South Sea Bill.

The company was fully investigated. The enquiry found the Company's books riddled with false entries. A report was presented on February 16, and many of Britain's leading politicians were found guilty. Some fled the country; others suffered public disgrace, or were even imprisoned. One took poison. It was a time of retribution.

The king's mistresses were, perhaps out of gallantry, not touched by the investigation. But the company's directors received little mercy. Their estates were confiscated by act of Parliament; and the money the State recovered went to the relief of their thousands of victims. As for the South Sea Company itself, it lingered on until 1854, when its £10,000,000 of capital was converted into government securities.

THE DREYFUS AFFAIR

The Dreyfus affair is one of the most flagrant legal scandals in history. The convicted man's innocence was suspected even before his trial, and was established shortly thereafter; yet it was to be years before Dreyfus was freed.

The true scandal behind the Dreyfus affair lay in the intense anti-Semitism of the nineteenth century French General Staff. Some Staff members considered Devil's Island an appropriate place for a Jew, guilty or not. Anti-Semitism was very strong in France in the nineteenth century, particularly among monarchists and right-wing factions who bitterly opposed the republican parties.

Napoléon had given the French people an exaggerated reverence for their army and its generals. The army was considered above criticism.

In those days the career of an army officer was within the means of gentlemen only. A commission in a crack regiment cost money. In England, where professional soldiers had been feared ever since Cromwell, the command of a fashionable regiment was sold to the highest bidder. This practice effectively excluded dangerous professionals and kept the army in the hands of aristocratic amateurs. In other European countries, too, the army was a gentlemanly career; money and family background advanced a man where talent and military skill could not.

Gentlemanly incompetence caused little damage as long as

THE DREYFUS FAMILY   *The Captain is shown with his wife Lucie, and their two children, Pierre and Jeanne.*

Europe did not face serious war. The era of the gentleman first yielded to the era of military efficiency in India as Britain's Imperial Indian Army faced serious fighting. Officers of the Indian Army were nevertheless looked down upon by officers of the home-based regiments, and the Crimean War brought considerable friction within the army itself.

In France the Revolution had swept away the feudal privileges of the great. Napoléon had democratized the army, promoting men according to their merit. "Every soldier carries a field-marshal's baton in his knapsack." But although Napoleon's memory was revered, his principles were not. By 1890 the French officer corps was proud and snobbish. Members of the General Staff were drawn exclusively from the Jesuit College in the Rue des Postes.

Alfred Dreyfus was born in 1859, the son of a wealthy, semitic, Jewish Mulhouse industrialist. Choosing the army as a career, he became a captain in 1889. After passing through the Ecole Suprieure de la Guerre, the college for Staff Officers, he received an appointment to the Ministry of War. He was the first Jew to presumably overcome anti-Semitic prejudice and become a Staff officer.

The appointment was extremely unpopular among his fellow officers. Dreyfus was disliked for reasons other than prejudice. He had an unattractive personality; he was dull, stiff, formal and unfriendly. Though he had inherited a large fortune from his father, he lived a modest, even frugal, life, free of the fashionable vices of his fellow officers.

In 1893 the French General Staff became aware of a spy in their midst. Secret military information was being regularly betrayed to the Military Attachés of the German and Italian Embassies in Paris.

French counterintelligence maintained contact with a janitress at the German Embassy, Madame Bastian, who every morning collected the contents of the wastepaper basket of

Colonel von Schwartzkoppen, German Military Attaché, and brought them to the French.

In September, 1894, this wastepaper basket produced, along with the usual rubbish, the famous *bordereau* which was to shake the world. This *bordereau* or memorandum, addressed to Schwartzkoppen, consisted of a letter enumerating certain military documents which the anonymous writer hoped to sell to Schwartzkoppen.

The *bordereau* read:

> *Although I have had no word indicating that you wish to see me, I am sending you, Monsieur, certain interesting items of information:*
>
> *1, a note on the hydraulic brake of the 120, and on the action of this gun; 2, a note on the covering troops (some changes will be made under the new plan); 3, a note on the change in artillery formation; 4, a note on Madagascar; 5, the draft of the Field Artillery Manual of Fire (March 14, 1894). This last-named document is very difficult to secure and I can have the use of it only for a very few days. The Ministry of War sent a fixed number of copies to the various corps concerned and these corps are responsible for them. Each officer who has one must return it after manoeuvers. Hence, if you will be good enough to copy anything that interests you and keep the original for me, I will call for it—unless you prefer that I make a copy in extenso and send you this.*
>
> *I am about to leave for manoeuvers.*

This communication fell into the hands of Major Hubert Henry. Henry was assistant to Colonel Sandherr, the Chief of Intelligence. Sandherr in turn was a super-annuated paralytic.

It was said that Major Henry recognized the handwriting of the *bordereau* as belonging to Major Esterhazy, a dissolute, illegitimate offspring of that famous Austrian family. Henry, a career officer who had risen from the ranks, was a man of considerable intelligence—or, as some wished it, of peasant

cunning. Whether or not he actually recognized the handwriting as Esterhazy's, he said nothing to those superiors examining the document. They somehow came to the conclusion that
it could only be the work of a Jew. There was only one Jew on
the General Staff; they reasoned he must be the traitor. Dreyfus was promptly arrested, though the evidence against him
was practically nonexistent.

This lack of evidence was obvious even to the most extreme
anti-Semite on the General Staff. Some Staff members moved
to drop the charge rather than make fools of themselves. But
Edouard Drumont, a violet anti-Semitic journalist, wrote an
inflammatory article stating that Jewish gold was being
offered in exchange for dropping charges against a Jewish
traitor. Certain newspapers then fell in line violently protesting the thought of a rich Jewish spy attempting to buy immun-
ity for his crimes.

The army authorities then decided they had no alternative
but to press their case against Dreyfus. Their only problem
was lack of evidence. Anxious to please his superiors, Major
Henry rose to the occasion. A practiced forger, as part of his
job was to produce false documents to be planted on foreign
agents, he provided sufficient faked evidence to condemn
Dreyfus.

Politically, Dreyfus' conviction grew more and more inevitable. The General Staffs of both Germany and Italy had
stated officially that they had had no dealings with Dreyfus.
But the French Minister of War, General Auguste Mercier,
staked his political reputation upon a conviction. Major Henry's career also depended upon it.

Despite the strong protests of the defense, the court-martial
was held behind closed doors. The court members, convinced of Dreyfus' guilt even before the trial began, anxiously
welcomed every scrap of evidence which might confirm their
conviction. They listened approvingly to Major Henry swear

in the witness box that a certain personage "highly respected," whom he could, of course, not possibly name, had told the French Intelligence Service that Dreyfus was the traitor. The

MADAME DRYEFUS   The wife of the defendant arrives at Rennes. She is accompanied by her brother and sister-in-law, Monsieur and Madame Hadamard. This illustration is from a photograph by Bouet.

defense naturally protested, asking that this mysterious person be named and give his evidence openly. Major Henry swore upon his officer's honor that what he said was true. This, for some reason, satisfied the court. They would doubtless have been shaken had they known that this "highly respected personage" was a small-time agent in the pay of French Intelligence, a Spaniard named Val Carlos.

Henry's *pièce de résistance* was handed to the court-martial when it was considering its verdict, supposedly behind closed doors. This sealed packet contained further alleged gleanings from the Schwartzkoppen wastepaper basket, including a letter containing the following sentence: "I enclose 12 Defense Schemes of Nice which that scoundrel D——— gave me for you. I told him that you did not wish to have anything more to do with him."

The forgery was crude, but it worked. The members of the court-martial considered the evidence conclusive. They were of course criticized for accepting evidence produced in secret without the knowledge of the defense, but they purported to believe that the matter was so secret and vital to the defense of France that they were justified in waiving the conventional forms of justice.

Found guilty by unanimous decision, Dreyfus was sentenced to be dishonorably discharged from the army and deported for life.

In such circumstances, the correct thing for a gentleman to do was to commit suicide. But Dreyfus was not the conventional gentleman. He steadfastly refused to do away with himself, much to the annoyance and embarrassment of the War Ministry. He was then promised reasonable treatment if he confessed. But he steadfastly maintained his innocence.

"My sole crime," he declared, "is that I am a Jew."

DREYFUS IN COURT   The prisoner, standing before the court-martial at Rennes, declares: "I am innocent."

General Mercier then ordered him sent to Devil's Island in stringent solitary confinement, with his papers marked "Hardened criminal. Unworthy of consideration." He was first publicly degraded in the courtyard of the Ecole Militaire, then taken directly to the convict ship. At Devil's Island he was treated with great severity, on the express orders of Paris. During the day a silent armed guard stood over him and at night he was chained to his bed. No one was allowed to speak to him.

With infinite relief the War Office closed this awkward and embarrassing case. It had learned its lesson: no more Jews would be promoted to the General Staff. But newspapers continued to search for Dreyfus' motive. He was rich, so it could not be money. They looked in vain for a woman in the case. The mystery seemed insoluble, unless it was a plot by international Jewry.

The actual treason did not end. Military secrets continued to find their way to the German Military Attaché. In March, 1896, the increasingly embarrassing Madame Bastian produced fragments of a letter written by Schwartzkoppen, but torn up undispatched, which was addressed by name to Major Esterhazy and which thoroughly incriminated him. Colonel Sandherr had by this time been committed to an asylum. His successor was Colonel Picquart, who had been promoted over the head of Major Henry—much to Henry's disgust.

Picquart, who had never been impressed by the case against Dreyfus, took another look at the *bordereau,* compared it with a specimen of Esterhazy's handwriting, and found them the same. Alarmed, Picquart laid this startling information before his superior officers, who were also alarmed but for different reasons.

They told Picquart the truth: they had no intention of reopening the Dreyfus case. The reputations of important people were at stake. Dreyfus himself was of no consequence.

Expert evidence on the writing of the Bordereau
M. Paraf-Javal demonstrating his theory on a black board.

HANDWRITING EXPERT *At the Dreyfus trial, M. Paraf-Javal demonstrates his theories regarding the authorship of the "bordereau."*

DREYFUS DECLARED GUILTY   *In the final scene of the trial, Colonel Jou-
aust delivers the verdict. This picture is from a sketch by artist-reporter Melton Prior.*

"What does it matter to you if this Jew is kept on Devil's Island?" Picquart was asked.

Picquart was outraged. He was promptly removed from his position before he could make any more inconvenient discov-

DISGRACE   In the ceremonial degradation of the convicted Dreyfus, his sword is broken and his buttons and insignia are stripped off.

eries. He was then ordered to the fighting area in Tunisia in the hope that a timely bullet would end his embarassing disclosures.

Major Henry was then promoted as Chief of Intelligence.

ANTI-DREYFUS PROPAGANDA   *"Dreyfus is a traitor," declares
the back poster. The superimposed front poster, like other propaganda
pieces of the day, hastens to blame Dreyfus for the most far-fetched misdeeds of the day. "Theft of cartridges and important documents at Fort
Vincennes. New treason by Dreyfus. Irrefutable proofs!" it reads.*

Henry expressed his thanks to the General Staff by producing a beautifully forged letter, supposedly from Colonel Panizzardi, the Italian Military Attache, which referred to Dreyfus in clearly incriminating terms. The delighted General Staff commended Henry and promoted him to colonel.

Meanwhile the Dreyfus family were fighting to clear Alfred's name. Picquart, in Africa, not yet shot, was in touch with a growing pro-Dreyfus movement in France. Esterhazy was accused of espionage, and the Schwartzkoppen letter forced him to face a court-martial. The court-martial, a brief farce, acquitted Esterhazy. Picquart, who had returned to France at his own request to give evidence, was arrested.

The pro-Dreyfus movement was not at full strength. Two days after the court-martial, Emile Zola's famous denunciation of the Dreyfus scandal appeared in Clemenceau's *L'Aurore* under the title "J'accuse." An open letter to the President of the Republic, it accused the War Office of committing a legal crime. Zola was prosecuted, found guilty and sentenced, and escaped to England. Picquart was dismissed from the army for insubordination.

The Dreyfus case, the government said, was now closed. It may well have been, but the scandal and controversy—*l'Affaire* as the French have ever since referred to it—was really just beginning.

The subsequent disaffection tore France apart. Public opinion was aflame. The anti-Dreyfusards were as numerous and fervent as the pro-Dreyfusards. Nearly everyone was committed to one side or the other. Families were divided, old friendships broken. There were innumerable duels and fighting in the streets. A press campaign broke out with extraordinary violence against those who believed Dreyfus innocent. Some said it was not a question of whether an individual was guilty or not; it was a question of the Jews and Protestants endeavoring to become masters of France. Anti-Jewish riots

Il y avait en 1894, à l'État-Major français, un jeune officier alsacien très savant, patriote et de bonne conduite appelé Dreyfus.

Par malheur, il y avait aussi, dans so reau, deux autres officiers : Du Paty de (et Henry, jaloux, intrigants, fourbes. Ils plotèrent de le perdre à la première occa

Les chefs, confiants en leur parole d'honneur, se laissèrent tromper et, croyant venger la patrie, condamnèrent Dreyfus.

Il fut condamné à perpétuité, mais le où on lui arracha ses galons, il cria fière « On dégrade un innocent, vive la Fran Et beaucoup de gens versèrent des lar

PRO-DREYFUS PROPAGANDA "The Story of an Innocent Man" appeared as a popular comic strip in 1898 or 1899, printed in Paris. The last owners of the drawings attributed this "Histoire d'un Innocent" to Georges Clemenceau.

INNOCENT

Paris. — Imp. Pochy

jour, un agent dévoué à la France réussit
ober un papier chez l'ambassadeur prus-
C'était justement une lettre d'un Français
ffrait de vendre sa patrie à l'Allemagne.

Du Paty et Henry en profitèrent aussitôt
pour faire croire à leurs chefs et à la France
que ce traitre était Dreyfus.

oilà quatre ans qu'un brave et honnête
cier alsacien, qui ignore pourquoi on l'a
damné, vit désespéré sur un rocher au
ieu du grand Océan.

Pendant ce temps, sa pauvre jeune femm
pleure toutes les larmes de son corps et se
deux orphelins crient : « Maman ! où es
mon papa ? »

*A contradictory account of the Dreyfus case was presented in other comic strips of
similar appearance, one of which was entitled "The Story of a Traitor."*

LE PIF
DU FRÈRE À MATHIEU

ANTI-SEMITIC CARTOON   A
caricature shows Alfred Dreyfus
on Devil's Island. "Le Pif" means
"Big Nose" or "Bottle Nose."

broke out. In Algiers Jewish property was looted.

France seemed on the edge of civil war. Responsible politicians tried in vain to calm explosive tempers and avoid controversy. Germany strongly resented its involvement in the scandal, and Berlin officially announced, if a bit naively, that their Intelligence Department had had no dealings with Dreyfus at any time.

Schwartzkoppen, compelled to silence by his diplomatic position, was reported bitter about the affair. After his death, his papers established that his dealings had been with Esterhazy, not Dreyfus. Esterhazy betrayed his country, it was revealed, to save himself from financial ruin. Reportedly, too, Esterhazy had gone to Schwartzkoppen offering important military in-

DREYFUS ON DEVIL'S ISLAND   "*The Meal*" *is one of a group of twelve
photographs showing the imprisoned man. The pictures are preserved in the collection
of B. Roussat, in Paris.
    In the top photograph the hut of the prisoner Alfred Dreyfus stands within the
stockade. At right are the buildings of the guards.*

J'ACCUSE . . . !   On January 13, 1898, Emile Zola's famous denunciation of the French Government over its treatment of Alfred Dreyfus appeared on the front page of the newspaper "L'Aurore." The accusation, which took the form of an open letter to the President of the Republic, stirred the conscience of France, and sold over 300,000 copies.

EMILE ZOLA   The French novelist and critic (1840-1902) is best known for his novels, which embody naturalist theories of literature, and for his continual involvement in controversial affairs—particularly the Dreyfus case.

Zola was educated in Paris where, in 1859, like many other distinguished writers, he failed his final exams. He spent the next two years job-hunting. Although some of the stories concerning this period—such as his having to stay in bed all day because he had pawned his trousers, or his subsisting by eating sparrows which he caught at his attic window—are undoubtedly exaggerated, it is true that Zola gained a first-hand knowledge of the life of the poor, through his own deprivation. Later, he drew heavily on this experience for his novels. At long last, he obtained a clerical job in a shipping firm—which he hated. He then moved to the sales department of a publishing house. Meanwhile, he wrote fiction. A volume of his short stories was published in 1864.

In 1866, his grim and sordid autobiographical novel, "La Confession de Claude," attracted the attention of the police, and his employers ordered him either to give up literature or quit his job. Whereupon he left the job, and supported himself as a freelance writer for the rest of his life. Some of his books, such as "Nana" and "Germinal," were attacked as pornography. But Zola always defended himself vehemently and ably against his critics.

Always involved in one controversy or another, Zola was one of the first to support the revolutionary impressionist painters of his time.

When the Dreyfus case became public, Zola was one of the first to declare that Dreyfus was innocent. On January 13, 1898, the newspaper "L'Aurore" carried Zola's open letter to the president of the Republic, which began with the words "J'accuse"—I accuse. The article, consisting of a series of assertions that for the most part were probably true but which were nevertheless insufficiently supported by argument or evidence, had such power that its denunciations reverberated around the world.

Zola was prosecuted for libel and found guilty. But he appealed and the sentence was quashed, and a retrial was held. Without waiting for the verdict, Zola fled to England. He died in 1902.

*SUPREME COURT OF APPEAL   In the last stages of the Dreyfus trial, the
Cour de Cassation prepares to hear M. Ballot Beaupre's report. From left to right,
the four robed figures are Beaupre, Reporter of the Case; M. Loew, President of the*

Criminal Chamber; M. Mazeau, First President; and M. Tanon, President of the Chamber of Petitions. This illustration, drawn from life by Paul Renouard, appeared in a contemporary periodical in June, 1899.

HEADLINES IN BUCHAREST   World-wide concern over the Dreyfus case is demonstrated by the "Mos Teaca, Jurnal Tivil Si Cazon," a periodical founded in Bucharest in 1895. Its issue of September 13, 1898 illustrates pro-Dreyfus agitation by Zola, Picquart, and others. This cartoon shows a skeletonized Alfred Dreyfus sitting on a seat made of the French newspaper "L'Aurore," being borne in a litter, by Zola in front and Labori in the rear. Colonel Picquart leads the march back to Paris. French army officers are shown fleeing in the distance.

formation if Schwartzkoppen would write a letter saying he had dealt with Dreyfus—a suggestion which the German was said to have rejected with great scorn.

Some historians have attributed the obstinacy of the French War Office to the involvement of someone much more important than Esterhazy; someone whose role they had to conceal. Many mysteries remain, and it is now widely believed that a second person was involved in espionage.

Henry's ruin was brought about by a new Minister of War, Eugene Caviagnac, who had the documents of the case re-examined. Henry's forged documents were discovered. Arrested, he did the thing expected of a gentleman—which by

UN DINER EN FAMILLE

(PARIS, CE 13 FÉVRIER 1898)

PAR CARAN D'ACHE

— Surtout! ne parlons pas de l'affaire Dreyfus!

... Ils en ont parlé...

A FAMILY DINNER   The celebrated French car-toonist, Caran d'Ache, illustrates the violence of opinion about the Dreyfus case. In the top picture, the father of the family says: "Above all, let us not talk about the Drey-fus affair." Below, the caption reads: "They spoke of it." This cartoon appeared in a French periodical on February 13, 1898.

AFFAIRE ESTERHAZY

Identité absolue des Ecritures

— ● ►—

Le BORDEREAU est l'œuvre du Commandant Esterhazy

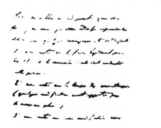
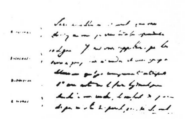

ESTERHAZY'S HANDWRITING   By juxtaposing portions of the treasonous bordereau with samples of Esterhazy's writing, this poster conclusively demonstrates Esterhazy's authorship of the document, and his guilt as both forger and spy. This unsigned and undated handbill is believed to have been printed toward the end of 1897, or in the early months of 1898.

the standards of the day he was not. He committed suicide. Esterhazy fled to England.

The authorities now had no option but to reopen the case. In June, 1899, Dreyfus was brought from Devil's Island and in August was retried by court-martial at Rennes. The trial lasted a month, with the old-evidence and the same false witnesses—all lying for the honor of the army. The court-martial finally gave its senseless verdict: guilty with extenuating circumstances. The sentence was ten years' detention. The world greeted the verdict with incredulous division. But the French Government understood that the army was merely refusing to admit its mistake. The decision saved them the embarrassment of prosecuting Dreyfus' army accusers.

Dreyfus was given a Presidential pardon, and in 1906 the Rennes verdict was reversed. Esterhazy had already confessed in 1900 that he had written the *bordereau*. He remained in England, where he died in obscurity in 1923.

Dreyfus served in the First World War and was made an officer of the Legion of Honour. He died in Paris in 1935.

"ESTERHAZY'S SECRET CONFESSION"   Undated posters such as this one, purporting to reveal new evidence pertaining to the Dreyfus case, only succeeded in complicating the mystery. This placard was printed at Asnieres by E. Nery for Leon Hayard.

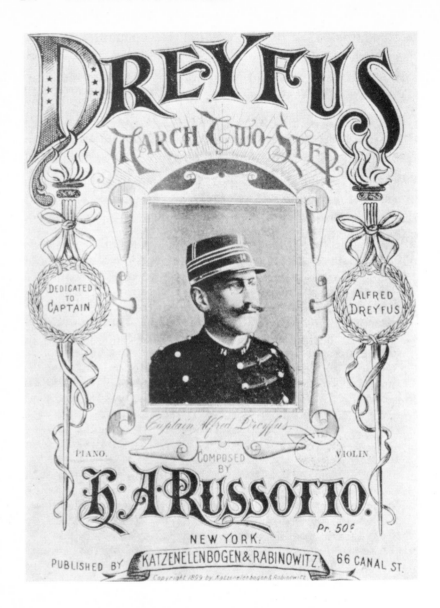

DEDICATED TO DREYFUS   Among many works of art and music created in honor of the victimized Captain Dreyfus was the "Dreyfus March Two-Step," composed by an American of Italian descent. Comparable expressions of sympathy derived from countries around the world.

The Dreyfus case had deep political consequences. Resultant waves of radicalism and antimilitarism brought radical government to France until the First World War. The case marked the end of the great prestige formerly accorded to the General Staff. The army became more democratic. A strong anticlerical movement lessened the influence of the Church.

The Dreyfus battle concretized an ancient conflict: the state versus the individual. The affair left behind it many mysteries, and it is by now thickly encrusted with legend. Some Frenchmen still believe Dreyfus was gulity; that he was freed by Jewish corruption and Jewish money. Most believe there were two traitors—Esterhazy and a highly placed unknown who complicated the case in order to escape detection. Some even believe that there was no traitor at all, that even the *bordereau* was a forgery, and that Esterhazy and Henry made up the matter wholly to frame Dreyfus. Others still regard Colonel Henry as a great patriot who gave his life for his country, and believe that his part in the affair was justified by national security. After his suicide a fund was collected to provide for his widow and children.

The whole truth may never be known.

TEAPOT DOME

The administration of President Harding, after the First World War, was undoubtedly the most corrupt the country had experienced since Grant's time. From it emerged the great Teapot Dome Scandal which, after the President's sudden death in 1923, caused a political upheaval which almost destroyed both the Republican and Democratic parties.

The two previous administrations, those of Taft and Wilson, had established national oil reserves for naval use. The one at Elk Hills, California, was known as Naval Petroleum Reserve No. 1; the second, nearby, was in Buena Vista Hills; No. 3 was at Teapot Dome, Wyoming. These rich oil fields were on government land and were set aside for the exclusive use of the United States Navy in the event of a national emergency. This policy, part of a larger conservation program, was opposed by many people, including, not unnaturally, oil companies who wished to exploit the oil themselves.

Teapot Rock is a large sandstone formation standing in the sagebrush flats of the county of Natrona, Wyoming. Although it looks more like a gigantic hand than a teapot, the word teapot stuck, and the petroleum experts who surveyed the area gave it the name Teapot Dome. This part of the county is a natural oil deposit, and in 1915 nine thousand acres of it were allocated for Reserve No. 3.

The chief figures in the Teapot Dome Scandal were ex-Secretary of the Interior and former Senator Albert B. Fall of

New Mexico; Presidents Warren G. Harding and Calvin Coolidge; oil millionaire Harry F. Sinclair of the Mammoth Oil Company; Edward L. Dohney of the Pan-American Petroleum and Transport Company; and Senator Thomas J. Walsh of Montana, the honest and hardworking investigator who exposed the scandal. Minor participants were legion.

Fall was looked on by some as the epitome of the corrupt Republican politician. Others saw him as a scapegoat for a wounded Republican Party. Neither of the two presidents came out well in the affair. Though perhaps untainted by corruption, they were justly blamed for their complacency. Harding showed to a restive United States an astounding executive incompetence, as well as a shabby, graft-ridden administration.

Harding, though inexperienced in national politics, was a man of great personal charm. Lacking in temperament, undistinguished in performance, the Senator from Ohio was propelled into the candidacy, almost because of these negative qualities. In 1920 he was swept into power on a tide of post-war disillusionment. His attitude of isolationist opposition to United States membership in the League of Nations found an echo in the hearts of millions of voters who seemed to have forgotten that the league was the brainchild of their own President Wilson. The Democratic Party was torn by internal dissension, and Harding won the election easily, securing 16 million out of the 25 million votes cast.

It was a time of great expansion for the United States. The population had risen from 92 million in 1910 to 106 million in 1920 and the national wealth from 180 thousand million dollars to 300 thousand million dollars during that period. Everywhere in the country business was booming.

Harding brought a number of strong men into his Cabinet —Herbert Hoover, Henry Wallace, Charles Evans Hughes, Andrew W. Mellon, and Will H. Hays. There were also some

*ALBERT B. FALL   The Secretary of the Interior had been a fron-
tiersman and a Senator from New Mexico. Here is how he looked before the Teapot Dome scandal broke, and before his health was broken.*

INVESTIGATOR Senator Thomas J. Walsh of Montana, chairman of the Senate Investigation Committee, was instrumental in uncovering the details of the Teapot Dome scandal.

less understandable appointments: the choice of Senator Albert B. Fall as Secretary of the Interior being the most obscure.

Fall was an American frontier baron with a rugged pioneering background. He had prospected for gold and silver in Mexico and the Southwest. A big landowner in New Mexico when it was still a territory, he had become prosperous. He was an individualist, a man of action, noted both for his courage and a tendency to take the law in his own hands. It was rumored that he had more than held his own in personal encounters with the gunmen and bandits of the old Southwest. Altogether, he was a flamboyant and picturesque character.

By profession Fall was a lawyer. When New Mexico was admitted to the Union in 1912, he ran for its first senatorial seat. While conducting his campaign he was accused of bribery and corruption, but he won the election. In Washington he continued to affect a large black Stetson, a string tie, a long drooping mustache—all of which powerfully contributed to his personal charisma as the rugged frontiersman.

Secretary of the Interior Gifford Pinchot, one of the most honored of United States politicians who had himself served many years in the Department, was to say that it would have been difficult to pick a worse man for the job than Fall. The position called for a man who had a "strong appreciation of public rights and interests." A frontier baron like Fall was hardly likely to be of this category. Whatever Fall's qualities might have been as a rugged American with a keen sense of elementary justice, he was obviously the wrong man for this particular job.

One of the important functions of the Secretary of the Interior was to administer the conservation of the nation's natural resources. From his first days as Senator, Fall had made clear that he was an exploiter and a friend of exploiters. His appointment alarmed conservationists.

In Washington, the controversy between those who wished to conserve natural resources and those who were determined to exploit them, was sharp and bitter. At the time, the incredible extent of America's natural wealth in petroleum was not fully appreciated by the public.

One of the first things that Fall did when he became Secretary was to reverse the policy on oil conservation. He persuaded President Harding to sign an executive order transferring the rights of the Naval Petroleum Reserves from the Department of the Navy into his own hands. This was done with the compliance of the Secretary of the Navy, Edwin N. Denby, who acted in good faith throughout.

It is impossible, however, to say the same for Fall. He might perhaps have had valid reasons for his belief that the nation's natural resources should be exploited rather than conserved, but his point that such expolitation would expand industry and increase economic wealth rang false. Fall was more concerned with his own interests than with those of the nation. Among his close friends were Doheny and Sinclair, both oil magnates and both eager to exploit the oil reserves in California and Wyoming.

OIL MAGNATE Edward L. Doheny, head of Pan-American Petroleum, was permitted to exploit a large tract of immensely profitable federal oil-reserve land—apparently in return for a $100,000 "loan" he made to Secretary of the Interior Albert Fall. Although Fall was found guilty of accepting Doheny's bribe, somehow Doheny himself was acquitted.

The transfer of the oil reserves brought immediate protests from naval officers and conservationists, and particularly Pinchot. Grave doubts, too, were cast on the legality of such a transfer.

In March, 1922, Harry A. Slattery, a prominent Washington politician, and an ardent conservationist who later became Under-Secretary of the Interior, discovered that Fall had leased a large tract of Reserve No. 1 to his friend Doheny of Pan-American Petroleum. Slattery entertained the gravest misgivings about the transaction, and he and Senator Robert La Follette of Wisconsin were of the opinion that Fall's activities should be closely watched.

On April 7, Fall leased the entire Teapot Dome area to Harry Sinclair's Mammoth Oil Company. This he managed by means of an executive order meekly signed by President Harding. Fall kept his mouth shut, but the news of the lease was reported on the front page of the *Wall Street Journal* on April 14. It was officially admitted by the Acting Secretary of the Interior a few days later, and was finally made public on April 21.

Washington by now was buzzing with rumors of scandal and corruption, and on April 22, La Follette voiced these suspicions in the Senate. His resolution calling for a committee to investigate the affair was unanimously passed on April 29.

The National Association of Oil Producers then stepped into the fight. On May 13, they protested to the Senate the irregularities in the development of the Teapot Dome oil reserve. They insisted the leasing was a "return to the era of land grabbing and carpetbagging whose hydrahead of iniquity was crushed by Roosevelt almost a decade ago."

For reasons which have never been made entirely clear, the Senate Investigation Committee procrastinated throughout most of 1923. Possibly they may not have believed that the matter was as serious as the rumors suggested. Meanwhile evi-

JUGGERNAUT.

CONSEQUENCES   A 1924 cartoon illustrates the political repercussions of the scandal.

TEAPOT DOME OIL FIELDS A view of the camp of the Mammoth Oil Company at Teapot Oil Dome, Wyoming.

dence which was to break open the scandal was being gathered by the Secret Service. It was a long and difficult task.

Fall doubtless knew what was afoot. On January 2, 1923, he suddenly resigned. The White House, in announcing his resignation, gave as the reason Fall's wish to devote all his time to his business affairs in New Mexico. Talk was that he had originally taken office "at great financial sacrifice." As there had been no question of forcing his resignation, Harding then offered him an appointment on the Supreme Court. Fall refused.

President Harding's administration was itself on the point of collapse. For months it had been under incessant sniping, accused of grave irregularities. Apart from Teapot Dome, there were stories of wholesale corruption in the Veterans' Bureau and in the Department of the Custodian of Alien Property.

Harding was finding that his easygoing geniality and personal popularity were not enough to run the country. Problems were pyramiding in every department. His administration was not only incompetent to deal with the problems, but was infiltrated by politically immoral men who could easily

mold the President to their wishes. Men close to the President were indulging in corrupt practices. Harding's laxness resulted in numerous abuses. The situation had become a scandal.

In June, 1923, Harding set out on a nationwide tour in an attempt to repair his administration's disfigured image. As the Presidential train progressed across the continent, he stopped to make speeches and meet the people. Their response was far from enthusiastic.

Indication that his loyal friends might bring discredit to him

COMEUPPANCE   In 1924, the Senate Investigation Committee holds hearings on the Teapot Dome scandal.

caused Harding great anxiety. He grew more and more distraught as the tour progressed. "I have no trouble with my enemies," he declared. "It is my friends who are giving me trouble."

In July, he went on to Alaska, where, it was reported, the receipt of a long cipher message from Washington almost prostrated him. Obviously under enormous strain, he nonetheless continued the trip to San Francisco. Specialists, called in by his own doctors, found him in a state of utter exhaustion.

He was taken seriously ill on July 28 and died suddenly on August 2, amid conflicting rumors and speculations on the cause of his fatal illness. Officially his death was attributed to an embolism.

Though Harding was himself free from corruption, he had trusted corrupt men and imprudently appointed them to positions of power. Their betrayal of his trust undoubtedly broke his spirit and contributed to his death. William Allen White described Harding's last illness as "part terror, part shame and part utter confusion," and said that it was "wickedly unfair" to saddle a man who was "weak, unprepared, with no executive talent" with the awful power and responsibilities of the President of the United States.

Vice-President Calvin Coolidge, who succeeded Harding at the White House, said years later that Harding "had discovered that some whom he had trusted betrayed him and he had been forced to call them to account. It is known that this discovery was a very heavy grief to him, perhaps more than he could bear."

Coolidge, a new broom, made no attempt to sweep clean the corridors of executive power. He believed his best course was to do nothing and the future was to prove him partly right.

Meanwhile the Senate Investigation Committee, under the chairmanship of Senator Thomas J. Walsh, began its quiet work. They became cognizant of a mysterious $100,000 acquired by Fall in circumstances which the former Cabinet officer was not prepared to disclose. In fact, he flatly denied that the money had anything to do with "Teapot Dome, or any oil concessions"—a direct lie that was to cost him dearly. Fall discovered, in the same way John Profumo did forty years later, that informal lying led directly to formal disaster.

The United States Secret Service had been probing into the mystery of the unexplained $100,000 and knew the names of

SINCLAIR OF MAMMOTH OIL   *Acquitted of conspiracy, finally, he was nevertheless convicted for contempt of the Senate.*

the two oil men concerned. The results of the investigation came as a bombshell.

In January, 1924, Edward L. Doheny went before the Senate Committee and testified that he was the man who had "loaned" Fall the $100,000. The little multimillionaire said that his son had taken the money to Fall's office in cash, in a black bag. Doheny produced a mutilated note which, he said, was the receipt signed by Fall, and asserted that he had torn off Fall's signature himself. He had done so in the fear that, should he predecease his old friend, Fall might be pressed by the Doheny estate to repay the loan at a time when it might be difficult for him to do so.

ATTORNEY GENERAL DAUGHERTY   Forced to resign under accusations of receiving payments and protecting criminals, Harry M. Daugherty always insisted on his innocence. Daugherty was born in Sullivan, Indiana, and had graduated from Wabash College. He was a Mason, a bank director, and a prominent Republican leader for over 20 years before his appointment to the Cabinet.

The scandal and sensation that followed Doheny's testimony was enormous. No one could escape now. Harding and his Cabinet were execrated. Even President Coolidge felt the guilt of association. He was accused of retaining in his administration men who had failed to "protect the public interests against a bunch of crooked oil operators."

With press and militant Democrats on the warpath and the public alarmed and outraged, it was useless for members of the Harding Cabinet to deny that oil leases had ever been discussed in the Cabinet. The political temperature was running so high in Washington that anyone connected with Teapot Dome was afraid of frying in their own oil reserve.

Further revelations pushed Fall deeper into the mud. Harry Sinclair of Mammoth Oil, who had been given the lease of Teapot Dome, admitted making Fall an unsecured loan of $25,000.

No longer could Coolidge ride the storm on the wings of executive serenity. Things were getting out of control. It was time, he decided, for a firm hand. On January 26, 1924, he issued a statement promising action against anyone who had committed criminal acts while entrusted with political power. "If there has been any crime, it must be prosecuted. If there has been any property of the United States illegally transferred or leased, it must be recovered." He took pains to point out that men of both political parties were involved in the scandal.

The Senate Committee continued to hold tense and exciting meetings. On March 23, Sinclair appeared before the Committee but refused to answer questions. He claimed that it had no powers to interrogate him about the lease. The Senate promptly asked for a grand jury indictment against him for contempt.

Sinclair, however, was not so closed-mouthed in other quarters. In Wyoming, reports went round that the Teapot Dome field had failed to yield anything like the quantity of oil that experts had predicted. Furthermore, Sinclair contended that he had spent $25,000,000 on it and would be glad to give up the lease. He had the gall to ask that he be reimbursed for his expenditure.

Fall, though sick and on the verge of a nervous breakdown, nevertheless appeared before the Committee where he took the Fifth Amendment as both petty and mighty crooks were often to do after him.

The political cauldron had now almost reached boiling point. Secretary of the Navy Edwin Denby, who had innocently if obligingly consented to the oil transfers, was forced against his will to resign. He left his office angrily protesting the accusations of malfeasance leveled against him.

The heat was then turned on Attorney General Daugherty, a friend of both Sinclair and Doheny, who was accused of having received payments from violators of prohibition statutes and of protecting criminals from prosecution. His resig-

EVIDENCE This note was Albert B. Fall's acknowledgment of the $100,-000 unsecured "loan" he received from E. L. Doheny. Fall's lies and denials, Doheny's voluntary mutilation of the note, the secretive delivery of the cash—all pointed to the true nature of the payment.

nation was forced by Coolidge and he, too, went with ill grace, indignantly denouncing his accusers. "To my dying day," he said, "I shall expect Mr. Coolidge to make an explanation of his action."

It was now the Democrats' turn to suffer. Doheny struck the first blow. He stated that during President Wilson's administration he had paid a retainer of $25,000 a year to William G. McAdoo, then Secretary of the Treasury, "to represent us in Washington in connection with Mexican matters." McAdoo, it was disclosed, had received a total of $150,000 for legal work rendered after he had retired from government service. McAdoo, at the time of the disclosure, was an active candidate and front runner for the 1924 Democratic nomination in the forthcoming presidential election.

Excitement ran high throughout the country as the controversy between the two parties reached a pitch of near-hysteria. Charge and countercharge were hurled with bewildering rapidity.

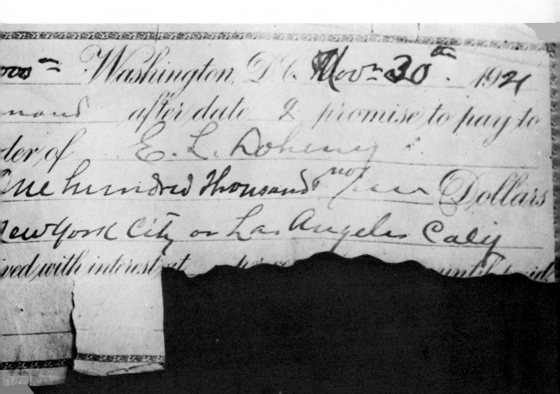

On February 11, McAdoo testified before the Senate Investigation Committee, vigorously denying "taint of any kind." His connection with Doheny, he insisted, had been purely as a legal advisor. McAdoo was not seriously damaged by the attempted smear, which apparently was more political than personal.

FALL ON TRIAL   His health broken by disease and strain, Albert B. Fall is helped into the courtroom in 1929.

Congress requested that court proceedings be undertaken to cancel the California oil leases granted to Doheny as well as the sale of the Teapot Dome fields to Sinclair. It followed this up by asking that criminal proceedings be instituted against Fall.

In the midst of the bitter partisan debates in the Senate, Senator Tom Hefflin enlivened the humorless harangue by breaking off in the middle of an attack on Doheny to read the following parody by James Henry of Leigh Hunt's poem "Abou Ben Adhem":

> *Abou Dough Heenie (may his tribe increase!)*
> *Awoke one night from a deep dream of peace*
> *And saw within the moonlight in his room,*
> *Making it rich like a lily in bloom,*
> *A Senator writing in a book of gold.*
> *Enormous wealth had made Dough Heenie bold;*
> *And to the Senator in his room he said:*
> *"What writest thou?" The statesman raised his head,*
> *And with a look which made Abou boil*
> *Answered, "The names of those who seek for oil."*
> *"And is mine one?" said Abou. "We will see,"*
> *Replied the Senator; but Abou Dough cheerily*
> *Responded in a still and softer tone,*
> *"Write me as one who loves to make a loan."*
> *The Senator wrote and vanished. The next day*
> *He came again—it looked like* Caraway—
> *And showed the names of those whom Fall liked best.*
> *And lo! Dough Heenie's name led all the rest.**

The Senate, never noted for its lack of vulgarity, roared its appreciation, and then Senator Henry Cabot Lodge retorted

* Quoted in *Teapot Dome: Oil and Politics in the 1920's,* by Burl Noggle (Louisiana State University Press, Baton Rouge, La., 1962).

with a scarcely less ugly parody on a Longfellow poem. Everyone had their conception of a good time.

The disputed leases were canceled and proceedings were
instituted against the oil companies. Fall and Doheny were
charged with fraud and bribery and Sinclair with contempt of
the Senate. Sinclair was acquitted of conspiracy, but went to
prison for contempt.

A maze of trials, mistrials, retrials, and appeals continued
for years against Fall, Doheny, and Sinclair. Sinclair's acquittal in 1928 on the conspiracy charge was greeted with
amazement in Washington. Senator Nye ironically commented that it provided evidence that you cannot convict a
million dollars in the United States.

In October, 1929, Fall was sentenced to a year's imprisonment for acepting a bribe, and was fined $100,000. He was
now a physical wreck, suffering from tuberculosis, as well as a
variety of other diseases. Both appeal and Presidential re-
prieve were refused, and he finally went to prison in Santa Fé
in July, 1931.

Although Fall was convicted of accepting a bribe from
Doheny, Doheny was found not guilty of bribing Fall. This
verdict was greeted with the observation that if you can't convict a million dollars, it is even less possible to convict a
hundred million dollars—the extent of Doheny's wealth.

Under United States law the offer of a bribe does not carry
the same penalty as accepting one. Nevertheless, Fall's conviction struck many as injustice in view of the fact that both
Sinclair and Doheny were acquitted. The Republican Party,
greatly damaged by the scandal, needed a scapegoat, and Fall
was viewed in that light by a large part of the public.

He left prison in May, 1932, penniless and a broken man,
abandoned by all his former associates and his multimillion-
aire friends. Only his wife stood loyally by him. The authorities released him from payment of the $100,000 fine imposed

upon him, on account of his penury. He died in 1944 at the age of eighty-three in an El Paso hospital surviving Doheny by nine years.

The immediate force of the Teapot Dome investigation died down almost as quickly as it arose. By May, 1924, it had been relegated to the inside pages of the newspapers. The country was beginning to grow bored with the scandal.

McAdoo remained an obstinate and active candidate for the Democratic nomination and came close to capturing it at the Democratic Convention in New York in July, 1924—the longest and fiercest in sixty years.

By November of that year the voters appeared to have forgotten the oil scandal, and it played almost no part in the election. It certainly did not damage the Republican Party in the eyes of the country: Coolidge was returned to power with a substantial majority.

THE SWINDLES OF CLARENCE HATRY

There is an English saying that the margin between prison and a peerage is often very narrow. The exploits of Clarence Hatry, early 20th century financial wizard, would seem to support its truth.

Hatry's friends have often represented him as an unlucky genius overwhelmed by circumstances beyond his control. On the other hand, many of his financial contemporaries had always regarded him as crooked, and would have nothing to do with any endeavor in which he was associated.

Hatry was born in Hampstead in 1888 and educated at St. Paul's School. His father was a silk merchant with a business near Cheapside. He died when Clarence was nineteen. Young Hatry took charge of the family business, which within eighteen months was in the hands of the Official Receiver—bankrupt. However, he was not held responsible for the bankruptcy; he was immediately released. His liabilities of £10,000 were legally quashed. Nevertheless, with one of his few outbursts of integrity, he paid back the money.

He then went into the insurance business. By 1911, when he was twenty-three, he was earning £20,000 a year. In the boom which followed the First World War he bought the Commercial Bank of London and went into high finance. He specialized in taking over failing concerns and infusing new life into them by means of mergers and reconstructions. By the time he was thirty he was a millionaire.

THE YOUNG CLARENCE HATRY With soulful expression and natty apparel, Hatry displays the high style that carried him through his multi-million-pound swindles.

Though Hatry did not make many mistakes, he followed his intuitions when purchasing a concern. He would casually visit a South Coast store, walk three times around the ground floor and say without asking to look at figures, "I don't bargain. I'll give you £300,000. Take it or leave it." He bought Leyland Motors from the Spurrier Brothers for £350,000, and the same day sold it for £600,000.

In the years following World War I, Hatry dabbled in every conceivable kind of commercial venture. He amassed huge capital gains. He owned several famous stores. He amalgamated a number of glass firms into British Glass Industries, and a number of Scottish jute firms into Jute Industries Limited. He owned a dressmaking business in Bond Street, and the *Globe* newspaper, not to speak of a number of racehorses, one of which won the Lincolnshire Handicap.

His fortune was estimated at between two and three million pounds. He lived in a splendid house in Grosvenor Square and he owned an estate in Sussex. Besides racehorses, he was master of a £40,000 yacht, the second largest in the world. It boasted a crew of forty and a saloon where twenty people could sit down to dine.

Hatry's extravagances were legendary. He gave his staff lavish presents. He tipped royally. He would walk along the Embankment at night distributing five-pound notes to derelicts.

The postwar boom did not last long. His financial empire soon began to totter. In 1923 the Commercial Bank of London was on the point of collapse, £750,000 in debt. To keep his businesses solvent, Hatry sold his homes, his yacht and his racehorses. Nearly all his personal fortune went into this retrenchment. Even his wife contributed £130,000 which she had saved from her pin money.

Hatry immediately set about rebuilding his empire. In 1924 he formed Austin Friars Trusts Limited, named after Austin

Friars, the London street its offices overlooked. He also floated Corporation and General Securities Limited to negotiate corporation loans. His aggressive cut-price methods made him many enemies in powerful financial circles, and some of these were to contribute to his eventual downfall.

He formed the Drapery Trust, which consisted of a chain of famous English department stores such as Plummer Roddis, Bobbys, Marshalls, Edwin Jones and Swan and Edgar. He sold this trust to Debenhams and was reported to have made a million pounds' profit from this deal alone.

One of his most important operations was the creation of Allied Ironfounders, a three million pound merger of twenty-three small firms in the light steel industry. He then created Steel Industries of Great Britain, an eleven million pound amalgamation of heavy steel concerns. His professed aim was to reorganize and eventually control the entire British steel industry.

Toward the end of the 'twenties a boom was on. Hatry was dealing in really big money; twelve million pounds a month was said to be passing through his hands. He bought another splendid London house, this time in Great Stanhope Street, now Stanhope Gate, off Park Lane. His friends were dazzled by the opulence of his private palace, with its Jacobean hall and Georgian ballroom complete with musicians' gallery. On the second floor Hatry installed a swimming pool so he could go straight from his bed to a morning dip. In the basement he built a full-scale pub in the Elizabethan style which he called Ye Olde Stanhope Arms.

By this time Hatry was up to his neck in shady deals. He formed a company called Secretarial Services. It performed many of the tiresome formalities connected with the transfer of shares and bonds for the industrial companies and local authorities with whom he acted. On many of these shares Hatry forged the signature of the company secretary con-

CLARENCE HATRY   The financier in 1929, about the time of his great crash.

cerned, thus creating dud shares, most of them in gilt-edge securities. The many investors who did not trouble to verify the signature of the company secretary were to regret their credulity.

During the amalgamation of his steel companies, Hatry invited some shareholders to exchange their shares for a new issue. Sir Gilbert Garnsey, head of Price Waterhouse, a man of great integrity in the financial world, was cited as trustee of this issue. Those who checked with Sir Gilbert discovered he knew nothing of the arrangement. Less wary buyers received phony shares and lost their money.

Hatry produced a telegram from the United States Steel Company which stated it would advance large sums to finance the steel amalgamation. On the strength of this telegram, Sir Arthur du Cros, founder of the Dunlop Company, advanced money to Hatry through his firm, the Parent Trust. The telegram was a forgery and du Cros lost several million pounds.

Hatry was unlucky as well as crooked. The great Wall Street crash was imminent. A world of unlimited credit and inflated share values was about to collapse and bring on the great Depression. The Hatry crash, when it came in 1929, was the biggest of the century. It involved thirteen million pounds.

Hatry's huge steel operation led to his downfall. To finance his proposed new corporation, Steel Industries of Great Britain, he needed to sell five million pounds' worth of shares. He needed three million more to pay off bank overdrafts.

It was "bridging finance", familiar to thousands of house buyers today, which wrecked Hatry's second financial empire. Hatry arranged bridging loans in various ways. He said that the late Lord Bearsted, head of the Samuel banking house, had agreed to lend him four million pounds against stock he was proposing to buy in the negotiations over United Steel. When the loan was called Bearsted denied making any such agreement.

Hatry insisted that he had a verbal agreement, like many London transactions. But there was nothing on paper, and when Lord Bearsted repudiated him Hatry had to raise four million pounds in three weeks.

HATRY'S HOUSE *The financier's palatial residence on Great Stanhope Street, West London, featured a basement pub and a second-floor swimming pool.*

The whole world seemed in financial trouble. There were warning signals from New York where the frantic boom was reaching its height. The 1929 Labor Government had just taken over in England, and London was uneasy at the prospect of socialist policies. Many foresaw a world depression, though few, if any, guessed how great that depression would be. Consequently, no financier would help this volatile and

SIR MONTAGU NORMAN The Governor of the Bank
of England astutely refused to lend money to Hatry.

brilliant man who was suspected of questionable financial practice, if not of downright fraud.

In the summer of 1929 Hatry and his fellow directors, Edmund Daniels and John Gialdini, worked desperately to avoid disaster. They needed the confidence of the city and failed to gain it. Hatry's shares began to slide. Hatry appealed to Montagu Norman, Governor of the Bank of England, for help. Norman refused him; and he advised other finance houses to do the same.

Hatry continued his frantic efforts to escape his predicament. Having dealt extensively in loans to local authorities, he printed huge quantities of Wakefield, Swindon and Gloucester stock scrip which he pledged to banks as security for loans of more than a million pounds. The banks then held security greatly exceeding the actual value of the issue.

The steel stock continued to fall. To support it in the market, Hatry needed more and more cash. More bogus scrip was printed. Discovery was inevitable unless he could somehow lay his hands upon the odd million. Hatry hoped until the end that he would find someone to back him.

The crash came in September. By the 17th of that month Hatry realized that he would not have the cash to meet his commitments. Gialdini had left for Switzerland, ostensibly to raise money. Hatry never saw him again. Hatry, Daniels and two other directors remained in England to face the consequences. Hatry asked his bank for an increased overdraft. The bank replied that the affairs of the Hatry group should be investigated.

London was alive with rumor. In one day the market value of Hatry's issued ordinary capital fell by £2,500,000. Hatry failed in his last attempts to sell United Steel to an American concern, and Sir Gilbert Garnsey was already officially investigating his affairs. Garnsey frankly advised Hatry to go to the police.

LORD BEARSTED After denying that he ever promised Hatry a loan, the head of the Samuel banking house (left) visits New York with his associates Herbert Samuel and Simon Manks.

On the morning of September 20, 1929, Hatry and his fellow directors made statements to Detective Inspector George Stubbings, while on the Stock Exchange the greatest crash in history was taking place. The plunge was so catastrophic that the Stock Exchange Committee suspended dealings. Hatry and his companions were arrested that evening.

Hatry was refused bail. At his trial, for fraud and conspiracy, before Mr. Justice Avory in January, 1930 his practices were revealed. To make up a deficiency of nearly a million pounds in one of his companies, he had raised £795,000 by means of forged bearer securities. He had withheld from

HATRY IN 1939   The swindler is shown upon his release from prison, after serving nine years of a fourteen-year sentence for fraud and conspiracy.

the municipal authorities of Swindon, Gloucester and Wakefield sums amounting to £822,000. He had duplicated shares by means of bogus transfers. He had swindled hundreds of small investors as well as the municipal authorities.

Justice Avory had no mercy. Sentencing Hatry to fourteen years, Avory said his defense was "the same as that of any office boy who dipped into the till to back the favorite."

Some criticized the sentence as being too severe. Others had no pity for a man who had apparently helped cause a national financial catastrophe. Some, exaggerating his importance, blamed him for the Wall Street crash which happened six weeks after his arrest.

Hatry served only nine years; he was released from prison in 1939. He had not wasted his genius while in jail. He had persuaded a friend to lend his wife some money to buy a block of his discredited steel stock. His intuition was right. A consortium acquired the steel stock and formed United Steel Companies. The stock soared and Mrs. Hatry made a huge profit.

When he came out of prison Hatry was not quite impecunious. His creditors were generous to him. During the Blitz he lived in an expensive suite at the Dorchester, and during air raids he was one of the few persons permitted to sleep in a cozy concrete cubical in the hotel's Turkish baths.

THE CRASH   After the sensational collapse of the Hatry Group stocks, a crowd collects outside the London Stock Exchange.

In 1939 he wrote a book detailing his plan to abolish wars and unemployment. During the war he became interested in the publishing business. He bought Hatchards Bookshop in Piccadilly for £6,000. After building up the business he sold it at a great profit. He bought a total of thirty bookshops, several lending libraries, four printing companies and the publishing house of T. Werner Laurie. By 1950 he controlled companies worth £1,7,000,000, of which his personal share was thought to be three-quarters of a million.

But things were not as prosperous as they appeared. Once more Hatry overreached himself. In 1952 he resigned from the board of Hatchards Associated Interests, reportedly suffering a nervous breakdown. In 1953 a bankruptcy petition against him was dismissed.

The old suspicions lingered. Hatry's association with any commercial undertaking was equivalent to the kiss of death. Most London firms would have no dealings with businesses with which he was connected.

He died in June, 1965, at Westminster Hospital after five coronary attacks. Hated by many, admired by some, even envied by a few, he was a man of remarkable, if misguided, talents.

THE ENGLISH PENAL COLONIES

During the reign of James I in the early 1600s, Britain conceived the idea of unloading its criminal population on its colonies. In the 1620s, a shipload of "a hundred dissolute persons" were disembarked at the settlement of Jamestown in Virginia.

Although most of the prisoners—prostitutes, debtors, and ne'er-do-wells—who were transported to America during the 17th century were sold on their arrival as indentured servants, not a few wound up as virtual slaves. Like the helpless Africans who were also transported to the New World in that era, the English criminals and undesirables were sold on the auction block on arrival.

When the Thirteen Colonies declared their independence in 1776, Britain was forced to look elsewhere for a place to unload its unwanted. Canada would no longer do. "It was not deemed expedient," one Briton explained, "to offer to the colonies that remained loyal in America the insult of making them any longer a place of punishment for offenders."

Presumably New South Wales, the fledgling colony in Australia, was not so prone to insult. To the 18th-century Englishman, Australia was located at the other end of the earth. No more distant and therefore no more excellent accommodation for England's undesirables could be conceived.

For many years Australia served as a most convenient dumping ground. Indeed, the founders of New South Wales

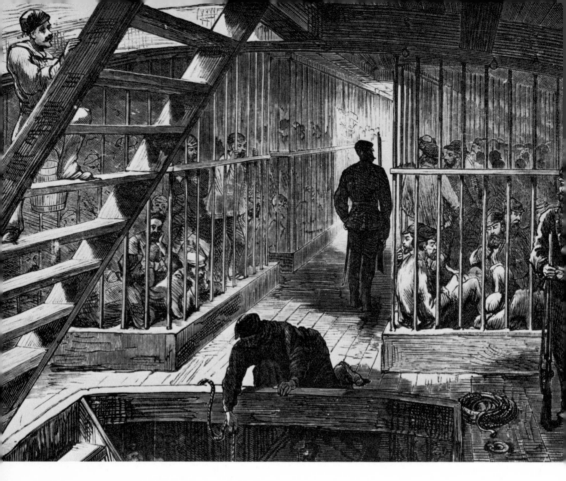

CONVICTS ABOARD SHIP   In the 1850's, a transport ship is crammed with ill-treated human cargo.

were none other than a cargo of convicts who arrived in 1788. In that year, a fleet of six ships hove to at Botany Bay, and deposited a pitiful lot of half-starved prisoners, 550 males and 192 females. This was the first of a long series of ghoulish shipments. More than 40 passengers had died on the way; and those who survived might have been better off had they succumbed en route.

The transports continued to arrive from England. Year in and year out, emaciated, skeletal men and women, chained two by two, shambled from the ships to their new lives in New South Wales. On some of these transports more than a quarter of the prisoners died at sea, most of them through slow starvation. Of course, there were scores of free colonists and troops for the garrisons who also made their way to the "new" continent, but a huge proportion of Australia's settlers were persons disgorged from England's prisons.

When the convicts arrived, they were often assigned to the free colonists as servants and laborers; but first choice went to members of the garrison, who whenever a new cargo of humans was anchored in the bay, went aboard to take such females as struck their fancy. So, as might be expected, there was a booming birth rate in Botany Bay—but very few marriages. Two-thirds of the children born were illegimate; and venereal disease ran rampant.

However, the worst convicts were not exported to New South Wales, but were sent to Tasmania, an island off the south coast of Australia, then called Van Diemen's Land.

The penologists of Van Diemen's Land had devised a peculiarly savage cat-o'-nine-tails lash; each tail consisted of a double twist of whipcord which contained nine knots. This flesh-ripping instrument was in daily use. One witness described how he saw a man staggering away from a flogging with the blood running down his legs and squishing out of his shoes at every step.

> *A dog was licking the blood off the triangles, and the ants were carrying away great pieces of human flesh that the lash had scattered about the ground. The scourgers' feet had worn a deep hole in the ground by the violence with which they whirled themselves round on it. The infliction was one hundred*

lashes at about half-minute intervals so as to extend
the punishment through nearly an hour. They had a
pair of scourgers who . . . (took turns with the whip)
and they were besplattered with blood like a couple
of butchers.

Guarded by ravenous dogs that were specially trained to attack on command, bound day and night in manacles and weighed down by heavy chains, the convicts of Van Diemen's Land were forced to wear yellow uniforms with the word "felon" printed from top to bottom. The prisoners occupied solitary cells at night, and were forbidden to speak to each other on pain of severe flogging. In Indian file, these silent, debased creatures set out each day to submit themselves to "the heaviest and most degrading labor that [could] be found." The slightest sign of reluctance was answered by the lick of the scourge.

However, Van Diemen's Land, horrible as its tortures were, was not the worst of the English penal colonies. That dubious distinction went to Norfolk Island, a South Pacific garden spot about 900 miles to the northeast of Sydney, Australia. This island, one of the most beautiful settings in all the world, the English had turned into a hell without equal.

"Intractable" and "irredeemable" men, including some who had survived their sentences in New South Wales only to be convicted again, were sent to Norfolk. In its heyday, the island boasted 70 soldier-wardens for a prisoner population of 300.

Convicts on Norfolk Island were burdened with heavy irons while they worked. Flogging triangles, iron gags, bridles, and headstalls (a most painful kind of head harness) were the order of the day. One of the most inhuman of Norfolk's torture devices was an iron frame called "the stretcher"; a man would be spread-eagled on this frame for 12 hours,

CHAINS   *Arm and leg irons, guns, chains and weights were all*
used to secure prisoners en route to the colonies. The ship is the
H.M.S. "Success."

with his head hanging back without support, and the prisoner would often die of brain hemorrhage if not of the sheer agony of the ordeal.

The single product of the Norfolk colony was cayenne pepper. The milling of this pungent spice was in itself one of the most fiendish of the tortures devised for the inmates. The stinging pepper dust on raw wounds drove the men mad with pain.

PRISON BARS   Aboard the H.M.S. "Success," iron bars secured the hatches and cubicles where prisoners were kept.

CHAIN GANG   Convicts at work in Van Diemen's Land, 1831. This illustration itself is an early example of engraving done by the remote and poorly-equipped colonists.

For most of the convicts of Norfolk, death was a blessed release. Prisoners entered bizarre suicide pacts; a man would kill his intimate friend and, the good and merciful deed accomplished, walk joyfully to the gallows. In one instance, 13 convicts arranged a revolt, knowing full well it had no chance of success. Their real goal was the gallows, and they went to their deaths with gladness.

A clergyman who had tended to the spiritual health of these men in their cells later delivered the following testimony to a Parliamentary Commission investigating conditions in the penal colony:

> *I said a few words to induce them to resignation, and then I stated the names of those who were to die;*

PRISON HULK   *Bound for the penal colonies, convicts board a transport ship in Portsmouth Harbor, 1828.*

CERTIFICATE OF FREEDOM.

No.

381/470

By Order of His Excellency Major General Sir RICHARD BOURKE, K.C.B., Captain General and Governor-in-Chief of the Territory of New South Wales and its Dependencies, &c., &c., &c.

THIS IS TO CERTIFY, that *Seven* Years having elapsed since Sentence of Transportation for that Term was passed on *Francis Neill* No. 31/663, was tried at *Dublin City* on the 19th of *July 1830* and who arrived in this Colony by the Ship *Waterloo (2)* *Addison* Master, in the Year *1831*, the said *Francis Neill* who is described on the other Side, is restored to all the Rights of a Free Subject under such Circumstances.

Given at the Colonial Secretary's Office, Sydney, this *Fifth* Day of *June* One Thousand Eight Hundred and *thirty-eight*

Registered in the Office of the Principal) Superintendent of Convicts.   }

CERTIFICATE OF FREEDOM   *After seven years of servitude, a convict was granted his freedom. His certificate was signed by the Governor of New South Wales.*

*and it is a remarkable fact that as I mentioned the
names of those who were to die, they one after another, as their names were pronounced, dropped on
their knees and thanked God that they were to be delivered from that horrible place, while the others who
were not to die stood mute and weeping. It was the
most horrible scene I have ever witnessed.*

The same clergyman also testified that prisoners on their
way to the gallows in the penal colony at Van Diemen's Land
were known to have paused on the scaffold to thank God
that they were going to their deaths instead of to Norfolk
Island.

A second witness who testified before the Parliamentary
Commission described a routine hanging of three Norfolk
convicts:

*Their execution produced a feeling, I should say,
of the most disgusting description. The convicts were
on that occasion assembled around the gallows for
the purpose of witnessing the execution, and so buoy-
ant were the feelings of the men to be executed and
so little did they seem to care about it that they absolutely kicked their shoes off among the crowd as
they were about to be hanged, in order, as the term
expressed by them was, that they might die game. It
seemed, as the sheriff described it more like a parting
of friends who were going on a distant journey on
land, than of individuals who were about to separate
from each other forever. The expressions that were
used on that occasion were, 'Goodbye, Bob!' 'Goodbye, Jack!' and expressions of that kind, among those
in the crowd, to those who were about to be executed.*

Some convicts at Norfolk were dehumanized to the point of complete insanity. One miserable creature who had been shipped out of England at the age of 13 for stealing a hare, had spent most of his years of punishment cooped up in a small cage. In old age he was grizzled, gaunt, half naked, and utterly mad—"a gibbering animal," one witness recalled.

Those who managed to escape from the penal colony in Van Diemen's Land often turned to cannibalism, once they had reached the wilderness. One John Barnes, a physician attached to the Van Diemen colony at Macquarie Harbor, testified that 116 convicts had escaped during the five years between 1822 and 1827. Of these, 75 had perished (presumably from starvation and exposure), two had been shot by the soldiers, eight had been murdered, one had been hanged for murder, 13 had been hanged for other reasons, 24 had been unaccounted for, and six had been eaten by their companions.

One member of a party of eight that escaped in September, 1822, gave himself up to the authorities a year later. All eight had resorted to cannibalism, and eventually six of the eight had been eaten. The survivor's last victim was found hanging from a tree, like a carcass in a butcher shop, eviscerated and ready to be devoured. The wretched survivor of the party was taken to the town of Hobart where the horrified authorities rushed him to the gallows.

It was not until 1837 that these dreadful facts came to light. For years before that time there had been rumors of the horror in New South Wales, but none of the rumors had been properly "confirmed." By the mid-1830s, however, Australians were asking if there were not some other place in the Empire to which the New South Wales colony might be removed.

By 1837, out of the total New South Wales population of

BOTANY BAY   *Captain Bligh, better known for his misadventures aboard the "Bounty," served as Governor of this convict settlement near Sydney, Australia.*

77,662, no fewer than 27,831 were convicts. In Van Diemen's Land the situation was even worse. Between 1831 and 1835, some 15,000 convicts had been deposited on that island and the complaints of the settlers could no longer be ignored.

A Parliamentary Commission was set up to examine the situation. Its investigation was thorough; and when it published its findings, the English public was outraged. It was obvious that the "transporting system," with respect to New South Wales, at least, had to be stopped at once. In the words of Edward Gibbon Wakefield, the great colonial statesmen of the day, "the unclean thing had got its death warrant."

Within two years, the transportation of felons to New South Wales was stopped, but Van Diemen's Land continued to bear its burden until 1852. At that time, the island authorities flatly refused to accept any more convicts from the home country. The Norfolk Island penal colony lasted four years longer—shutting down, finally and forever, in 1856.

HARRY THAW: MURDERER

On the evening of June 25, 1906, New Yorkers were served a spicy, after-dinner crime that was to provide them much delectation for months to come. The case of "the girl in the red velvet swing" (as it was to become known throughout the country) had all the elements that a sensation-loving public could desire: wealth, beauty, fame, sex and sexual deviations, glimpses into the lives of actors and of the very rich, topped off with a touch of English nobility. What happened could not have been more simple or more final. In the presence of Evelyn Nesbitt Thaw, and hundreds of spectators, at the opening night of a new revue in the Madison Square Roof Garden, Harry Thaw shot Stanford White to death.

The backdrop was New York City at the turn of the century. This was the heyday of the Gay White Way, the Forty-Second Street Country Club, Rector's, the Café des Beaux Arts, and the reigning beauties of *Floradora*. It was the day of Diamond Jim Brady, Lillian Russell, Florenz Ziegfeld, and *The Belle of New York*. This was a period in which the wealthy openly sought diversion. The artist James Breese gave a dinner party that concluded with a dessert in the shape of a huge pastry pie. From the middle of the pie, canaries rose and flew to every corner of the room as a fifteen-year-old girl in diaphanous costume broke through the pastry. (Stanford White was one of the guests.) It was said that at another party a beautiful naked showgirl sat in a bath of champagne from which gentlemen drank with silver ladles.

Against this background, the drama of Evelyn Nesbitt Thaw, Harry Thaw, and Stanford White was played to its conclusion. The murder was done with great deliberation, and Thaw turned to his wife afterward and walked toward her, holding up his pistol for all to see.

There are various versions of what she said to him on that memorable occasion. "My God, Harry, what have you done?" is one of them. To this he is supposed to have replied with exemplary calmness, "It's all right, dearie, I have probably saved your life." And to the policeman who appeared almost immediately, Thaw said, "He deserved it. He ruined my wife, and then deserted the girl." Evelyn declared: "Harry, I'll stick by you."

Thaw was promptly charged with first-degree murder, the penalty for which was death. Evelyn was as good as her word (up to a point).

It all began in 1901 when the beautiful sixteen-year-old Evelyn Nesbitt, a member of the *Floradora* chorus, met both Stanford White and Harry Thaw.

No one enjoyed the opportunities offered by turn-of-the-century New York more than Stanford White. White was an eminent architect, respected for his significant contributions to the architecture of the city. A bon vivant who enjoyed fraternizing with actors and directors, he entertained them lavishly in his studio eyrie on the top of Madison Square Garden Tower. He was partial to beautiful young showgirls, and with money enough to indulge his taste, he was rarely seen without at least one fresh, young beauty clinging to his arm.

In the scandal which erupted at his death, White was accused of the large-scale deflowering of New York City virgins. So spitefully envious of White's sexual reputation was Thaw that when he visited Domremy, the birthplace of Joan of Arc, he wrote in a hotel visitors' book that Joan of Arc would not

"MAD HARRY" THAW Heir to five million dollars, the young playboy spent lavishly on girls. He is shown here before his marriage.

have remained a virgin for long had White passed that way.

Was White just another libertine, or was his fondness for pretty girls the exterior sign of an interior sickness? It is easy to raise such questions; more difficult to answer them. Certainly Stanford White enjoyed many feminine favors. His conquests may have been facilitated by the fact that girls who entered the theater in those days did not expect to lead virtuous lives. The case got its name from a famous appointment in White's studio; a red velvet swing, on which the feminine guest swung up to the ceiling, dangling her pretty legs for the delectation of the would-be seducer below.

In contrast to Stanford White, who was one of the distinguished architects of the twentieth century, Harry Kendall Thaw accomplished nothing creditable in his long life. He was the oldest son of the late William Thaw, a railroad and coke magnate who bequeathed forty million dollars to his widow and heirs. The Thaws, like many turn-of-the-century *nouveaux riches,* had been unsuccessfully endeavoring to buy a place in American aristocracy. They were, however, more successful in their efforts to purchase a toe-hold in English society, an effort

STANFORD WHITE   Whatever the truth about his personal life—whether he was a corrupt roué or merely a swinging man-about-town—White was an exceptionally prominent architect, and a member of the most successful and influential architectural firm in United States history. White, carefully trained as a draftsman, had an instinct for decoration that was inspired. In 1879, he joined Charles Follen McKim and William Rutherford Mead to found the firm of McKim, Mead and White. In its early years, the firm excelled at informal buildings, such as the Casino in Newport, Rhode Island. After 1885, the firm championed the formal traditions of Renaissance architecture. White's designs included several of New York City's most famous landmarks: the Century Club, the Herald Building, Madison Square Presbyterian Church, and Madison Square Garden.

which was crowned by the marriage of Alice Thaw, on April 21, 1903, to the impecunious Earl of Yarmouth, the heir to the Marquess of Hertford. There were drawbacks to the marriage: the earl was arrested for unpaid debts on his wedding morning and the wedding was delayed while the Thaws paid the creditors off and made a million-dollar settlement on his lordship. With the exception of Harry Thaw, who drew the line at the open purchase of a husband for his sister, the Thaws considered the marriage a social triumph for the family. They proudly made frequent visits to the countess at the Hertford ancestral home. As the Thaws saw it, the marriage was one in the eye for Mrs. John Jacob Astor and company of New York City, who looked down their aristocratic noses at the upstart Thaws.

In the tradition of the age, Harry Thaw was a fabulous spender. The five million he inherited from his father allowed him to be. On one occasion in Paris he entertained a hundred courtesans at a lavish dinner party at which each lady found a piece of jewelry next to her serving place. That little item of entertainment cost him $50,000. In his courtship of Evelyn, he relied on such tasteful touches as sending her roses entwined with fifty-dollar bills.

At thirty, his life was crowded with dull, unoriginal pranks, such as riding his horse up the steps of his club and making ridiculous scenes in public places. "Mad Harry" was one of the kinder epithets bestowed on him.

The ill-fated marriage of Evelyn Nesbitt and Harry Thaw took place on April 4, 1905. It is never safe to presume that cupid presides over the marriage of a society scion and a beautiful showgirl, and this union seemed no exception. It is said that Thaw married as much to please his mother as for any other reason. Mrs. Thaw senior had been putting pressure on her son to settle down. So far as his mother was concerned, any marriage—even to Stanford White's cast-off mistress—

EVELYN   *Miss Nesbitt as a demure young beauty—the image she sought to perpetuate throughout her husband's trial.*

THE OTHER EVELYN   This touseled pose suggests the wanton side of Evelyn Nesbitt's personality—undoubtedly the force that drove her husband to murder.

was better than the disordered life of his bachelorhood. As for Evelyn, it seems likely that her desire to acquire a wealthy husband was stronger than her discrimination.

The early weeks of their married life were not uneventful: they managed to get themselves ejected from a famous New York hotel to the accompaniment of much publicity. Subsequently they settled down with Mrs. Thaw senior in the Thaw mansion in Pittsburgh, where local society refused to receive the former *Floradora* girl. Their first wedding anniversary behind them the young Thaws, on that fatal June evening, were placidly making plans to sail to England to join a family party. Mrs. Thaw senior had already left on one of her frequent visits to her daughter, the Countess of Yarmouth. News of White's murder awaited Mrs. Thaw on her arrival in England. She immediately reembarked for New York, much against the advice of her daughter, for whom the killing spelled social doom.

Thaw money quickly went into action. In New York City, the Thaw family lawyers were planning an insanity plea in the hope of getting Harry quietly away to a private institution which would provide him with those comforts suitable to his pocketbook and social position. After all, the New York Penal Code stated that a criminal act committed by an insane person is not a crime: the definition of insanity stated that it was to apply to a person "laboring under such a defect of reason as either not to know the nature and quality of the act he was doing, or not to know that the act was wrong." The difficulty hinged on the decision of state medical officers who advised that Thaw was legally responsible.

In prison the necessity to organize his defense did not occupy all of Thaw's time. Not satisfied with murdering White the man, he did his best to murder White's reputation too. He got in touch with Anthony Comstock, the president of the Society for the Suppression of Vice, an organization that had

SCENE OF THE CRIME On an opening night at the Madison Square Roof Garden, before hundreds of spectators, Harry Thaw shot Stanford White.

made itself faintly ridiculous by its over-puritanical campaigns.

As the result of what Thaw said to him, Comstock issued a statement saying that after what he had been told about White, he believed that Thaw had been prompted by the "purest motives." Comstock added that "Thaw thought White

was a monster who ought to be put out of the community."
This Thaw had done, most effectively.

With the return from England of the formidable Mrs. William Thaw, willing and able to take up cudgels on her son's behalf, the campaign to assassinate White's character moved into high gear. She promptly employed a highly paid publicity agent to present her boy Harry to the press as a Sir Galahad defending the honor of his wife; a simple, innocent girl who had been debauched and ruined by the unspeakable Stanford White.

Mrs. Thaw senior declared that she was prepared to spend a million dollars to save her son's life, and it was soon evident that she was not going to let a small thing like the truth stand in her way. The handling of Mrs. Holman was early proof of this.

Evelyn's mother, Mrs. Holman, had seen nothing of her daughter since Evelyn's marriage. This had been one of the conditions laid down by Mrs. Thaw. Now Mrs. Holman came forward with an offer to vindicate the character of Stanford White, whom she had known in the days when Evelyn was his protegee. There were letters in her possession, said Mrs. Holman, that would throw a different light upon the relationship between Thaw and White. They would prove, among other things, that Thaw never had any intention of marrying Evelyn and did so only reluctantly and under duress. There was never any reason for Thaw to be jealous of White, "who treated Evelyn as he would have treated a daughter—with the utmost respect and consideration."

Mrs. Holman declared she would pass the letters on to the district attorney and that she would go into court as witness for the prosecution. But she changed her mind after a visit from Mrs. Thaw's attorneys, who then issued a statement saying that Mrs. Holman would not give evidence after all. It seemed that she was in a "delicate state of health."

It was said that Mrs. Holman was better off by $50,000 as a consequence of her "delicate health," and that she had been trying to sell the letters to the Thaw family all along, but that the Thaws would not pay her price. It took a public statement to make Mrs. Thaw realize that Mrs. Holman's price was not too high after all.

Never one to suborn by halves, Mrs. Thaw paid to have the police records of Harry Thaw's past crimes and misdemeanors destroyed. Everyone who had something to sell was abruptly in business. Whitewashing Harry Thaw became, for a while, a thriving business.

While awaiting the Thaw trial, New Yorkers were entertained with a crude melodrama at the Amphion Theatre, Brooklyn, which dramatized the story of the White murder. The hero of this piece was Harold Daw, and the heroine was Emeline Hudspeth Daw, though one wonders, in terms of the plot, why the author had troubled to change the names. The lascivious villain was predictably named Stanford Black. This unspeakable wretch made a suitable entrance by savagely knocking down a blind old man who was demanding to know what Black had done with his innocent (and beautiful) daughter. Not even the girl-in-the-pie episode was left out, and the murder was staged exactly as it had taken place.

"No jury on earth," cried Daw from his prison cell as he awaited trial, "will send me to the chair, no matter what I have done or what I have been, for killing the man who defamed my wife. That is the unwritten law made by men themselves, and upon its virtue I will stake my life."

The play's backer was Mrs. William Thaw.

But the Thaws did not have it *all* their own way. Evelyn Thaw's reputation was being subjected to newspaper gossip columns. It was said that Evelyn had been seeing White as recently as two weeks before the murder.

More gossip, vouched for by Florenz Ziegfeld, reported that on the day of the murder three showgirls called at White's studio. They left after finding White out. "Just say Mrs. Harry Thaw called," one of the girls said mischievously to White's butler. When White returned and got the message, he promptly sent Evelyn flowers and a note of regret that he had missed her. It was said that Thaw found both flowers and note a few hours before he shot White.

Finally, the case was called before the Criminal Branch of the Supreme Court of New York.

Special arrangements were made for the press. The trial was to be covered in papers all over the world. The courtroom was packed. Only the privileged were allowed in and that did not include the general public. The Thaw family had a private room in the court and their own special seats. Mrs. William Thaw, a stately white-haired dowager, was dressed in black and wore a veil. The Countess of Yarmouth is supposed to have arrived for her brother's trial with a message of sympathy from Queen Alexandra herself.

The trial began on January 21, 1907. Quarterback on the defense team was Delphin Michael Delmas, a famous courtroom performer known as the Napoleon of the Western Bar. He was a small man with a magnificent voice who had secured nineteen acquittals out of nineteen murder cases. The Thaws had employed five other attorneys: John B. Gleason, Clifford Hatridge, Daniel O'Reilly, George Peabody and Hugh McMink. The lawyers were divided among themselves as to what was the best defense. Some favored an insanity plea; Delphin Delmas found himself inclined toward a defense based on the unwritten law. The Thaws had already decided that, despite all their enormous bribes, Harry stood little chance of getting away with murder by relying on the unwritten law. His only chance was to plead insanity. Delmas, who was supposed to head up the defense team, disagreed.

The district attorney for the prosecution was William Travers Jerome. (His cousin Jennie Jerome had married Lord Randolph Churchill and was the mother of Winston Churchill.)

The trial was formally opened by Assistant District Attorney Garvan. He was brief and to the point. After describing the murder he said: "The People claim that this was a cool,

DELPHIN MICHAEL DELMAS In defending Thaw, the famous lawyer achieved his 20th acquittal in 20 murder cases. Known as "the Napoleon of the Western Bar," Delmas was skilled in courtroom dramatics. He was a powerful orator and knew how to manipulate witnesses. Under his careful guidance, Evelyn Thaw gave one of the most memorable courtroom performances of the century.

MAMA AND THE COUNTESS Impressively dressed for her son's trial, Mrs. Copely Thaw arrives at court with her daughter Alice, the Countess of Yarmouth.

deliberate, malicious, and premeditated taking of human life. After proving that fact to you, we will ask you to find the defendant guilty of the crime of murder in the first degree."

The defense did not dispute the facts of the murder, and the case for Thaw was opened, to the surprise of everyone, by John Gleason, a lawyer who had had little criminal experience. Apparently, he was now senior man in the Thaw legal setup.

Gleason said: "We will prove that Harry Thaw was insane when he killed Stanford White, that he killed Stanford White under the delusion that it was an act of Providence, that he was the agent of Providence to kill Stanford White. The defendant killed Stanford White because he did not know that that act was wrong, because he was suffering from a disease of the brain which induced that condition of mind under the expansive operations of which he believed it was right to kill Stanford White, acting under the influence of his insanity."

Gleason's disorganized ramblings, of which the above is but a sample, was a gloomy foretaste of things to come. His handling of the medical experts he called upon to sustain his insanity plea was little short of disastrous. District Attorney Jerome tore the doctors to shreds in cross-examination. He pressed one doctor, a defense witness, to admit he did not know what the coccyx was and to confess ignorance of the nervous system. One doctor said that Thaw's remark to Evelyn after the shooting ("I have probably saved your life") indicated that he was acting under a delusion. Jerome asked him witheringly: "Do you consider that everyone who is actuated by jealousy is of unsound mind?"

Gleason's inept performance had badly hurt the defense team. Delmas threatened to withdraw from the case unless given complete charge of the defense; his stand was backed up by the other four attorneys. Gleason had no choice but to step down.

ROGUES' GALLERY   Police files contain these photo-graphs of Harry Thaw.

Delmas proceeded to call to the stand the stage-door keeper at the Madison Square Theatre. The keeper said under oath that he had seen Stanford White produce a gun and swear that he would kill Thaw before daylight. Jerome was unable to shake the testimony of this witness.

On the following day Evelyn Thaw was called to the stand. In anticipation of this event the biggest crowd ever drawn to a New York murder trial had gathered outside the court building. She wore a plain dark-blue suit and a shirt-waist with a schoolboy collar fastened with a black bow. She looked sixteen, instead of twenty-two. The newspapers were to remark upon her melancholy, radiant beauty, and her demure appeal. One wrote that she looked as "tiny and helpless as an aggrieved child," and "her voice was high and childlike, yet full of emotion."

PRISON FARE   Even in jail, Harry Thaw was provided with a tablecloth, a cut glass pitcher, and other amenities. He is shown here before his trial.

She gave a wonderful performance. Under the expert coaching of Delmas, she climbed the heights of courtroom histrionics.

Softly, she told the story of her father's early death and her mother's struggles to make ends meet. At fifteen, she had become an artist's model. (In those days this usually meant posing in the nude.) Then, at sixteen, she had joined the *Floradora* chorus.

Delmas had some difficulty in getting the state to allow her to relate to the court the story of her relationship with Stanford White, which, the state upheld, was not relevant to the issue. But she was permitted to tell what she had told Harry

ON THE STAND   Wavering between claims of insanity and the "unwritten law," Thaw answers questions.

Thaw about the relationship, because the defense claimed that it was this story which had impelled him to murder White.

Evelyn began her account with a trip to Europe in 1903, in which she and her mother were Thaw's guests. It was unconvincingly denied that she went as Thaw's mistress. Apparently, she was not deterred by the fact that she was already White's mistress and was regularly receiving money from him. Thaw proposed marriage to her in Paris. She told him at that time that White had seduced her and she had been his mistress for some time. The stage was now set for what New York, and half of the world, had been waiting months to hear: the story of Evelyn's seduction by Stanford White.

It had begun in August, 1901, when Evelyn started to visit White's studio. White seemed to have no difficulty in persuading her to amuse herself on the red velvet swing. Then one evening, in September of that year, she found herself alone with White in his rooms. The others "had not turned up," she said. After showing her some of the beautiful things in his apartment, he took her to an upstairs room which contained a curtained recess. Within it was a bed. After drinking some champagne with White, she passed out.

"When I woke up," Evelyn told the court, "all my clothes had been pulled off me and I was in bed. I sat up and screamed. Mr. White was there, and he got up and put on one of the kimonos. I pulled some covers over me and sat up and saw there were mirrors all around the bed. There were mirrors on the side of the wall and on top. Then I screamed again and he came over and asked me to keep quiet, that I must not make so much noise. He said, 'It is all over. It is all over.'" She paused here for the horror of what had happened to sink in fully. "Then I screamed again," she continued, "and cried, 'Oh no! Oh no!' Then he brought a kimono over to me and went out of the room. Then, as I got out of bed, I started to scream more than ever."

In answer to Delmas, eager to wring every drop of emotion out of the situation, she emphasized that when she regained consciousness she found White, naked, in bed beside her. She said White knelt beside her and told her that she must not be worried about what had happened. Everything was going to be all right. He would do a great many things for her.

"He said he thought I had the most beautiful hair he had ever seen. He said I was so nice and young and slim, and that he couldn't help it, so he did it. He told me that only very young girls were nice, and that the slimmer they were, the prettier they were. He said that the great thing in this world was not to be found out. He said that all women did this kind of thing, but the wise ones were not found out." Did the girls in the *Floradora* sextet do these things? Evelyn remembered asking. White laughed and said it was a good question. "I don't remember how I got my clothes on, or how I went home," she said, "but he took me home. Then he went away and left me and I sat up all night."

The revelation that she had only White's word that the dreadful deed was done, was too delicate a matter to be pursued in court.

Thaw became very excited when she told him this story. He cried: "Oh God! Oh God!" He bit his nails and sobbed desperately.

Evelyn and Thaw then quarreled over what had happened. She told him that "she had been to a great many apartments with Stanford White," and that she did not think it would be right for she and Thaw to marry. "He kept saying that he could not care for anyone else and that his whole life was ruined."

It was a most satisfactorily dramatic morning. Everyone, including the accused, was moved by the recital of the bedroom scene. The women in the court were apparently hanging their heads in shame as well as hanging on to every word

JURY RECESS   *During a break in their deliberations, the
jury in the Thaw trial stretch their legs.*

Evelyn said. Evelyn herself was drained by her emotion-
packed performance and tottered, "sobbing weakly," to the
Thaw private room. "The best actress in America could not
have done it as well," said one seasoned reporter.

Leaving Thaw in Europe, Evelyn returned to New York
City, where she renewed her intimacies with White. Her relationship with White at this time and after her marriage, how-

ever, was delicately ignored by her under Delmas' skillful questioning.

At this point, according to Evelyn, she was told by Stanford White and his friends that Thaw not only took drugs but was a sadist who liked to whip pretty girls. She was told that Thaw had once put a girl in a bath and poured scalding water over her. Evelyn said she believed none of these stories. Delmas hoped to lessen the impact of these shocking details by having his witness deny material that he was sure Jerome would bring out in cross-examination.

But again, according to Evelyn, White did not stop at amoral defamation of Thaw's character. He also took her to a crooked lawyer named Abraham Hummel, who specialized in devising blackmail schemes by which showgirls could extract money from wealthy men. Evelyn claimed that she was *made* to sign a statement saying that, during the 1903 European holdiay, she had been forcibly carried off to an Austrian castle by Harry Thaw, where she was forced by Thaw to submit to intercourse and was unmercifully beaten with a whip. The statement also said that during this painful holiday she had also discovered that Thaw was a cocaine addict.

Abraham Hummel, as a prosecution witness, testified that Evelyn had told him she had *not* told Harry Thaw that Stanford White had fed her drugged champagne and ruined her. She had sworn to Hummel, he claimed, that, despite Thaw's urging, she had refused to bring these charges against White because they were not true. Hummel's unsavory reputation

SECOND ACT   In fine clothes paid for by the Thaw millions, Evelyn appears for her husband's second murder trial in January, 1908.

was such that he was treated mercilessly in cross-examination, and his story was not taken seriously by the court or the public.

Under cross-examination, Evelyn steadfastly denied that there was any truth in the statement Abraham Hummel claimed to have taken from her after her European trip.

It soon became evident that the crux of the case was what Evelyn had actually told Thaw on that European trip.

Evelyn finished her defense testimony to the sympathetic applause of a shocked and scandalized nation; a nation avidly reading accounts of the testimony under such newspaper headlines as "The Vivisection of a Woman's Soul."

Evelyn's performance under the hostile cross-examination of the district attorney was equally brilliant. In vain, Jerome did his best to discredit her testimony. She was superb. Under his merciless questioning she more than once broke down and sobbed, evoking the jury's sympathy. She resisted all suggestions that she was a tarnished, experienced woman of the theater.

But Evelyn's defamation of White did not go wholly unchallenged. A showgirl Evelyn had mentioned in her testimony (she had accompanied Evelyn to White's studio on several occasions) made some frank comments that put the supposedly innocent Evelyn in a very different light. According to this colleague, Evelyn Nesbitt was known as a singularly provocative artists' model. Her colleague also pointed out that Evelyn Nesbitt, as a member of the sophisticated company of *Floradora,* knew very well what to expect when she accepted invitations from White and his circle.

The revelation that Evelyn had been cited as corespondent by the wife of a show-producer in which Evelyn played a gypsy girl (this was before she met White) was yet another reminder of the frailty not only of Evelyn's story in court but probably of Evelyn's morals. This was also true of her admission, forced out of her by Jerome, that she had undergone a mysterious operation "not countenanced by all surgeons."

Brilliant as it was, Evelyn's performance was less successful in cross-examination. Jerome did manage to destroy the image of Evelyn Nesbitt as an innocent and virtuous maiden wronged by a lecherous roué.

It was said that Evelyn was paid $200,000 for her performance in the witness box. Working in the *Floradora* company had never been so profitable.

It was now becoming clear that the whole case was to revolve around one question: Had Evelyn indeed told Thaw, that night in Paris, the story of her seduction by White as she

PROSECUTOR AND DEFENDANT William Travers Jerome (with paper in pocket), District Attorney for the prosecution, is shown with Harry K. Thaw. Man at right is unidentified.

testified she had? The prosecution's case was that the affidavit that Evelyn was supposed to have made to Hummel was the truth; that Thaw, by his cruelty, had indeed forced her to confess to White's infamous seduction. What was important was Thaw's mental state: not Evelyn's assaulted maidenhood or White's supposed debaucheries.

Then, to the confusion of all concerned, especially the somewhat baffled jury, District Attorney Jerome admitted there was a legal possibility Thaw was insane.

Thaw added to the confusion by issuing a statement to the

press: "I am not crazy. I was not crazy when I shot Stanford White. I'm glad I did it. I was justified when I shot him. I was never insane and never said I was."

Now, everyone was bewildered.

Jerome called Mrs. William Thaw to the box, and she spoke of a strangeness that settled over her son after he heard Evelyn's story of how White had treated her. Mrs. Thaw ad-

INSANE   Harry K. Thaw (left) is shown with the jury that declared him mentally unbalanced.

mitted that she agreed to her son marrying Evelyn on the condition that the girl's unsavory past "should be considered as a closed book, that it should be never opened and discussed."

At one point the defense called in a procession of psychiatrists (then called alienists) to give their opinion on Thaw's sanity. These gentlemen all pronounced the accused insane to a greater or lesser degree at the time of the shooting. This was what they were paid to say. One of them said Thaw told him he had no intention of shooting White, but that he meant only to bring him to justice. "But Providence intervened."

The judge then appointed a lunacy commission to examine the defendant. To the disappointment of the Thaw family, the commission declared Thaw sane and capable of instructing his counsel.

The trial drew to a close. In a two-day summation to the jury, Delmas poured forth torrents of sentimental oratory. The treacle may have covered up the fact that Delmas was trying, on behalf of his client, to both fish and cut bait—Harry Thaw had been provoked into exercising the unwritten law, and yet Harry Thaw was insane. Delmas tried to persuade the jury that Thaw suffered from a species of insanity known from the Canadian border to the Gulf of Mexico. Delmas called it *dementia Americana*. "It is that species of insanity which persuades an American that whoever violates the sanctity of his home or the purity of his wife or daughter has forfeited the protection of the laws of this state, or any other state."

Jerome appealed to the jury's common sense. He begged them to exercise this despite Delmas' "indecent appeal to their passions."

"This is no case of a St. George rescuing a maiden. This is a mere common, sordid, vulgar, everyday Tenderloin homicide, and you know it. This is a case where a woman lay like a tigress between two men, egging them on. To Thaw she said White had wronged her. To White she said Thaw had beaten her with a whip. Will you acquit a cold-blooded, deliberate, cowardly murderer because his lying wife has a pretty girl's face?"

Although posterity tends to agree that Jerome's analysis was correct, the jurors could not see the case in such stark lines. They could not agree on a verdict. Seven of the jurors found Thaw guilty of first-degree murder; five declared him insane and therefore not guilty in a criminal sense. The case would have to be tried again. Bail was refused.

The new trial began in January, 1908. The defense, which was one of simple insanity this time, was now handled by Martin W. Littleton. Again, District Attorney Jerome prosecuted.

Medical evidence was produced to show that Thaw was a manic-depressive, and the Thaw family doctor said the Thaw family had a history of mental imbalance. Again, Evelyn went on the witness stand. Again Evelyn, word for word and gesture for gesture, told the same story.

The defense was successful. This time the jury found Thaw not guilty on grounds of insanity.

But the jubilation of the Thaws was nipped in the bud by the judge. Since a manic-depressive is never completely cured, and since Thaw was "a person dangerous to the public safety," the court would order Thaw to remain permanently in the custody of the Asylum for the Criminal Insane at Matteawan.

Thaw was bitterly angry when he found that he faced incarceration after all. He was as sane as the next man, he claimed. The Thaws then began a long series of actions to free him from the asylum. The struggle went on in the courts from May 1908 until July 1915 without any success.

In August, 1913, Harry Thaw escaped from Matteawan and fled to Canada. That government, however, was not disposed to give asylum to an infamous murderer, no matter what his wealth and social credentials, and eagerly returned him to the

LOVING MOTHER Shown with her son Russell, Evelyn Nesbitt Thaw adds a new role to her repertory.

states. Escaping the death penalty with due process of law had cost him a million dollars, two prolonged trials, years of confinement in an asylum, and months of being hunted as a criminal and shunted from state to state. Finally, in July 1915, Harry Thaw was declared sane and released from confinement.

CHORUS LINE   Miss Nesbitt, in long skirt and horizontally striped blouse, rehearses for the opening of her night club, "Chez Evelyn," on West 52nd Street in New York City.

*COMEBACK   Returning to vaudeville, Evelyn Nesbitt opens
in an Atlantic City cabaret.*

During these court actions additional unsavory information
emerged. A former bawdy-house keeper in New York City
testified that she had rented rooms to Thaw so that he might
whip girls in the nude. During the murder trials $40,000 in
hush money had been paid out to these girls.

In 1915, when Thaw was declared sane, he and Evelyn,
who had returned to the stage, got the divorce they both
wanted. Thaw had killed for Evelyn's sake—so he claimed—

but the act did not bind the two together with ties of enduring love. Evelyn solaced herself by marrying her dancing partner. After an undistinguished career in vaudeville, she retired modestly to California. She later admitted that in her testimony she had embroidered and exaggerated the facts of her

RETURN TO BROADWAY   At the age of 52, on June 16, 1937, Evelyn makes another comeback, this one at "The Wivel." Miss Nesbitt is shown in her dressing room before her performance.

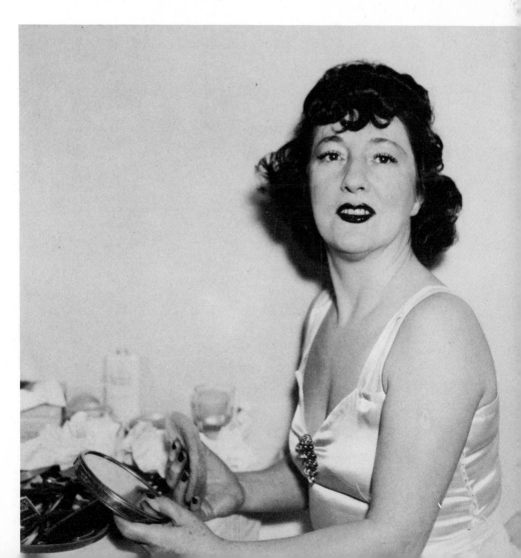

OLD AGE   Battered by a lifetime of scandal, jails, and asylums, Thaw arrives in Grand Central Station. He died in Miami in 1947 at the age of 76.

seduction by Stanford White. She said she had not really done all that screaming, though she *had* cried; Delmas had asked her to exaggerate her horror and shock. She admitted that it was White she really loved. She also admitted that she had made the statement to Hummel as *he* had claimed, and that the information about Thaw whipping her in Europe and her knowledge of his drug addiction was quite true.

Thaw lived to the ripe old age of seventy-six. Every now and then he emerged into the limelight. His passion for flagellation remained unabated, and he seems to have developed a taste for homosexuality, for in 1917 he was accused of whipping a nineteen-year-old Kansas City youth. After being committed to a mental institution on the old charge of insanity, he was again freed by a jury. Evelyn said she was not surprised at the most recent verdict. "There was dirty work at the crossroads."

Harry Thaw died in Miami in 1947. Few lamented his passing.

District Attorney Jerome seems to have been accurate in his analysis of the case at the first trial. Evelyn was guilty of trying to make Stanford White and Harry Thaw jealous of each other. She was guilty of being determined to marry a wealthy man. If she could not get marriage from Stanford White, whom she loved, she would get it from Harry Thaw, whom she did not love. Unfortunately the smoldering emotions she fanned most effectively were those of an unstable psychopath. Basically the girl in the red velvet swing murdered the man she loved.

CHILD LABOR

The terrible conditions under which children were exploited in the factories of Britain during the early 19th century were scandalous. That a civilized society could condone horrors perpetrated so visibly and on so grand a scale seems nothing short of monstrous. When the brutality of the child labor system finally reached the conscience of Britain's middle class, society recoiled in shock and anger. It was this reaction which led directly to the 19th century's outburst of radicalism, for it was the hideous injustice of child labor which inspired Karl Marx, in his book *Das Kapital,* to pillory the English industrial system.

In those days, anyone in need of a servant had only to apply to one of the foundling hospitals. Some little orphans went to relatively good homes; others, far less fortunate, lived out their lives at the mercy of cruel masters. All in all, the 18th century presents a grim picture of victimization of the young.

Spinning and cloth-making under the "cottage system" of that time was so profitable that every child in the household helped in the process. That meant hard work with a will, a will often reinforced by the parental rod. The whole family was involved in manufacturing, but the child remained under the roof of his parents.

But in the early years of the 19th century, machines began to take the place of cottage looms. As mechanical power superseded handskills, more and more artisans found them-

selves forced to leave their homes for the factories. In the
meantime, employers were discovering that machines could,
in many cases, be worked efficiently by children under the
supervision of an adult overseer. It was also discovered that
child labor was cheaper than adult labor.

At first, the children were mainly recruited from Poor Law
institutions. The practice was to use the "bothy system." A
bothy was a dormitory into which the children were herded
and locked up at night, like so many pack animals.

The children never saw a clock; therefore, they never knew
how long their hours were. They simply described them as
"unmercifully long." Through frequent beatings children were
forced to work without rest. So exhausted were they that they
often went to sleep at their machines, certain to be awakened
by the overseer's whip. After a long day's work, they were
herded back to the bothy. In the morning, the master would

Cable Wheel

come to the bothy, take up a pail of water, and throw it over those who were not out of bed.

The wretched children, kept under lock and key, were guarded by adults or older hardened children. Those who did escape were hunted down, brought back, and viciously flogged.

Perhaps the worst of these mills was owned by a man named Braid, who forced some of the girls to have sexual relations with him. His overseer, whose duty it was to thrash the children by day and by night, said that one winter morning he came across Braid kicking a girl along the floor. She had refused his advances, and she was bleeding at the mouth and nose. Other girls saw no point in refusing, and a number of orphans who slaved for Braid became pregnant. His wife and children were also living in this hellish establishment.

As the new industrial system grew apace, parish work-

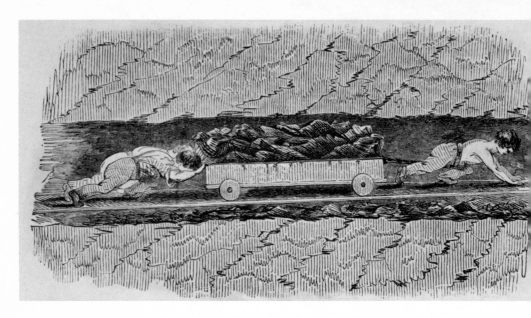

IN THE COAL MINES   Children move carloads of coal. Passages were often only sixteen to eighteen inches high.

houses were soon drained of children. The mill owner's demand for child labor increased.

After the Napoleonic Wars, a great expansion took place in the cotton industry. There were no longer enough orphans to fill the needs of factory owners. During the first two decades of the 19th century, some 300 thousand people migrated to Lancashire, the heart of Britain's textile industry. Many were children whose parents deliberately moved to Lancashire to take advantage of the great demand for child labor.

The adults themselves had little opportunity to secure employment. The status of the father as breadwinner weakened. Moreover, since they entered factories at the age of eight, and sometimes even younger, few children became trained for a trade.

British society of the day saw nothing wrong in the employment of children. The children of the poor had always worked; labor was considered good for body and soul. It was not realized at first that working at home under the supervision of parents was much different from working in a factory under the supervision of a paid overseer.

For the most part, the owners were men of meager education and rough upbringing. As a matter of course, the children were oppressed by their new masters, whether the employers were mill owners or mine owners.

INDUSTRIAL ECONOMY   An 1845 cartoon illustrates the effects of child labor.

SHAPE-UP On a Monday or Tuesday morning in 1850, children assemble to be hired for the following week. Under police supervision, girls of nine or ten years old were employed to clean, wash, tend children and cook for families that were luckily in work and required temporary servants. Wages ranged from one shilling to one shilling and fourpence a week, with no food given. This neighborhood, Spitalfields, was the district of the silk weavers in London.

England's prosperity during much of the 19th century was based on mining and cotton. The greed of the post-Industrial Revolution capitalist was one of the most destructive forces ever to affect English history. This greed destroyed family life, wrecked the health of thousands of children, and created all manner of social evil. Conditions did not exist in the same degree either in Europe or in America. Indeed, it is reported that an English overseer employed in a French factory considered the factory discipline to be lax. When he tried to introduce English work standards a riot ensued, which was quelled only by the calling out of troops.

SORTING SLATE   This illustration by Joseph Becker shows slate-pickers in the Pennsylvania Lehigh mining region in 1887.

By the 1820s, conditions in English factories had become truly grim. It was not until 1832, however, that questions were asked in Parliament. Some heavy, black leather thongs were exhibited, "the smack of which, when struck upon the table, resounded through the House."

Richard Oastler, a Yorkshire farm agent, nicknamed "The Factory King," led the crusade on behalf of the oppressed children. His newspaper article on "Yorkshire Slavery" exposed the prevailing abuses, and created a sensation. Oastler wrote that a West Indian slave master had visited a Bradford spinning mill, and after watching the children at work, had said: "Well, I have always thought myself disgraced by being the owner of black slaves; but we never in the West Indies thought it was possible for any human being to be so cruel as to require a child of nine years old to work twelve and a half hours a day; and that you acknowledge is your regular practice."

The Bradford mill owners offered no reply, but it is not recorded that the reproach made them lighten the burden on their little employees.

Witnesses told Parliament that toward the end of the long day, the crying of tired children being punished to keep them awake could always be heard above the clatter of the machines. Oftentimes, these children had been at the mill since four in the morning and were worked until nine and ten at night, with but sparse rest periods. Some were paid as little as three shillings (60¢) a week. A boy of 16 might work 82½ hours a week, which meant working right through Monday night and Friday night. For this gargantuan labor he was paid a sum equivalent to $1.50. Some boys had a work week which ran to 90 hours.

Unfortunately, parents often had no choice but to send their children to the factories, for the authorities would not give relief handouts to destitute parents with children who were considered old enough to work in the mills.

Nor was there any future for a child who had grown up in a mill and had ruined his health. Working for long hours in hot, humid air containing cotton particles which clogged the lungs afflicted many children with asthma. Other youngsters became deformed as a result of the unnatural postures they were forced to adopt during their work. Ill-nourished

PAYDAY   *At an inn adjoining the brick works,*
the brickbakers receive their wages.

little bodies were fashioned into pathetic shapes by the endless labor at remorseless machines, until finally the children broke under the strain and were unable to work at all. Thrown on the scrap heap, they were granted no compensation of any kind. Assisted by sticks and crutches, these maimed children crept before the Investigation Committee of Members of Parliament to tell their terrible stories. Many, overcome by

drowsiness at the end of a brutal day, had been mutilated by the primitive, unfenced machinery they had leaned on or fallen into. Some children had lost their fingers; others had had an arm torn off.

In 1832, on a typical day of hearings, one Parliamentary committee received the following testimony:

> *Hebden, William: age 19; Examined June 13, 1832*
>
> *Where do you live?——At Leeds.*
> *Are your father and mother living?——No; they are dead.*
> *What time did you begin to work at a mill?—— When I was six years old.*
> *What sort of mill?——A woollen-mill.*
> *Whose?——Mr. John Good's, at Hunslett.*
> *What were the hours of work?——We used to start at five and work till nine at night.*
> *What time had you for dinner?——Half an hour.*
> *What time for breakfast and drinking?——A quarter of an hour at each end of the day. . . .*
> *How were you kept up to your work during the latter part of the day?——The overlooker used to come with a strap, and give us a rap or two, or if they caught us asleep they would give us a pinch of snuff till we sneezed; they would give us a slap with a strap if we did not mind our work.*
> *Was the strap an instrument capable of hurting you badly?——It was a heavy strap, with a small handle to it.*
> *Where did they strike you with it?——Generally in the small of the back, and over the head.*

Did they strike the young children as well as the older ones?——Yes.

And the females as well as the males?——Yes.

State the effect upon your health of these long hours of labour?——I was pretty fair in health, but happened with two or three misfortunes.

State, in the first place, the effect upon your health and limbs of those long hours of labour? ——It produced a weakness in my knees; I was made crooked with standing the long hours.

Just show the gentlemen your limbs.

[The witness exhibited his limbs to the committee, which appeared exceedingly crooked.]

Are you quite sure you were, as a child, perfectly straight and well formed?——Yes.

How old were you before your limbs began to fail you?——About eight years and a half old.

Had you any other brother or sister working at the mill?——Yes; I had two sisters and a brother.

Have those long hours of labour had any effect upon the rest of your family?——Yes; upon one of my sisters.

Is she crippled?——She is nearly as bad as I am.

Was she originally perfectly straight and well formed?——Yes.

To what age did she continue to be perfectly well formed?——Till she was about nine years old.

How tall are you?——About four feet nine inches.

Are you quite certain that the deformity of your limbs was not consequent upon the accident you had?——No; it was not owing to that.

You were deformed, as you are now, before that?——Yes.

*Were the children unhappy at the state in which
they were?——Yes, they were.*

*Have you seen them crying at their work?——
Yes.*

*Had you time to go to a day-school or night-
school during this labour?——No.*

Can you write?——No, not at all.

Had you to work by gas light?——Yes.

*What effect do you think that has upon your
eyes?——It nearly made me blind; I was forced
to go into the infirmary; I was seven weeks there,
and the doctors said, towards the latter end of the
seven weeks, they did not expect they could cure
me.*

*What do you do now?——I sell potatoes.**

Black though the evidence was, the employers were by no
means repentant. It was asserted that the prosperity of the
cotton industry had saved England from famine. The inhuman
labor that crippled children for life should, they claimed, be
therefore viewed as a blessing; for such sacrifice had saved
these very children from famine.

One employer wrote lyrically of the delights of child labor:

*They seemed to be always cheerful and alert, taking
pleasure in the light play of their muscles; enjoying
the mobility natural to their age. It was delightful
to observe the nimbleness with which they pieced
the broken ends as the mule-carraige began to*

*Charles Wing, *Evils of the Factory System Demonstrated by Parliamentary
Evidence*, London Saunders and Otley, 1837.

recede from the fixed roller beam, and to see them at leisure after a few seconds' exercise of their tiny fingers, to amuse themselves in any attitude they chose till the stretching and winding-on were once more completed. The work of these lively elves seemed to resemble a sport in which habit gave them a pleasing dexterity.

FACTORY CHILDREN   A plant for the manufacture of colored paper. A factory similar to this one inspired Sarah Cleghorn's famous four-line poem:

> The golf links lie so near the mill
> > That almost every day
> The laboring children can look out
> > And see the men at play.

Some modern historians have minimized the horrors of child labor in the cotton industry. But although some reformers were guilty of exaggeration, the scandalous abuses were widespread and evident. Public opinion became thoroughly aroused.

It was Lord Ashley, later the seventh Earl of Shaftesbury, who was the leading spirit behind the Factories Act of 1833, which stipulated that children under nine were not to be employed in factories; that those under 13 must not work more than eight hours a day; and that those under 18 not more than 12 hours a day. The Factories Act, the Magna Carta for English children, became the base for other reforms designed to protect the young.

The plight of the boy chimney sweep had also aroused great concern at this time. In 1817, the House of Commons appointed a Select Committee to inquire into the employment of young boys as chimney sweeps. The abuses that were exposed were no less horrible than those which had been uncovered in the mills.

The chimneys of early 19th century Britain were swept by little boys who climbed up the flue and scraped the soot down with their arms and hands. Since no boy would undertake such disagreeable work of his own free will, it can be assumed that cruel coercion was used, a supposition which the Select Committee proved beyond doubt.

In 1803, a society was formed for the abolition of child labor in chimneys. This organization presented a grim and depressing report to the Select Committee. Boys were sold by their parents to master chimney sweeps for anything from three to five guineas ($15 to $25). The boys were maintained by their masters in the most shocking squalor, given soot bags to sleep on.

Boys of five and six were used for sweeping the narrowest chimneys. Some master sweeps employed their own children, sending them up chimneys at the age of four. There were estimated to be some 500 boy sweeps in London, hobbled

EXPLANATION   *"Well, we wanted to give 'im a chawnce, and was 'avin' 'im trained for a butterman, when wot does the beggar do but chucks it, and says as it's* CHIMBLEY-SWEEPIN' *as 'is 'eart was in!" So reads the caption of this ironic cartoon, from an 1897 issue of "Punch."*

boys who were readily identifiable to the general public by their emaciated appearance and knock-knees. Their education had been completely neglected. Not more than 20 of them could write their names; almost none could read. When they reached 16, they were too big to climb and, being unemployable, most of them took to a life of crime. Not surprisingly, they suffered from a variety of disfiguring skin diseases.

Master sweeps paid higher prices for smaller boys, since they could climb up the narrowest chimneys. The employers advertised that they had small boys "accomplished in the art of ascending flues and stove chimneys."

The Select Committee was informed that boy sweeps were subject to noxious sores on the thighs and knees as the result of their work. After a while, their elbows and knees became as calloused as the heel of a barefoot savage, but at first, boys forced to do this work suffered agonies. Witnesses spoke of boys being flogged to make them go up a flue. Straw was lit in a fireplace to drive the unwilling to ascend higher. A neophyte might be followed up a tall chimney by an experienced boy who would stick pins into the learner's feet if he did not ascend quickly enough.

"SUFFER LITTLE CHILDREN TO COME UNTO ME
A stirring cartoon from the demised "Life" magazine c
1914 protests factory conditions.

Medical evidence was introduced which depicted in grisly detail the nature of the childrens' deformities that were the direct result of climbing chimneys when growing bones were pliable.

> *The knees and ankle joints mostly become de-formed in the first instance from the position they are obliged to put them in order to support them-selves, not only while climbing up the chimney, but particularly in coming down, when they rest solely on the lower extremities, the arms being used for scraping and sweeping down the soot in the mean-time; and this in addition to carrying heavy loads confirms the complaint.*

Boys driven up by a ruthless master frequently became stuck in a narrow chimney and were unable to move. Some-times part of a chimney had to be removed to extricate a trapped child, who might be suffocated by the soot before he could be reached.

In May, 1813, a sweep named Griggs, with an eight-year-old apprentice, went to a brewery in Upper Thames Street to sweep a small chimney. A fire was still burning and the flue must have been nearly red-hot, yet as soon as he had ex-tinguished the fire below, Griggs forced the boy in from the top of the chimney. It was soon apparent that, owing to the heat of the chimney, the boy could not descend more than a few feet. Griggs called him to come up and out, but the boy was stuck and could not move. The lad's screams and cries were to no avail, as he was slowly roasted to death while a bricklayer made desperate attempts to get him out. At the inquest, the jury said the boy's death was due to "misfortune."

Notwithstanding that public opinion was seriously moved by the scandal of the chimney sweeps, it took many years before the practice was finally abolished. The chimney-sweeping trade could not easily be persuaded that it was more efficient to sweep chimneys with a long circular brush. In 1834, boys under 10 were prohibited from climbing chimneys; six years later, the age was raised to 21. But these laws were ignored for many years, and indifferent magistrates neglected to enforce them.

ON THE GALLEY   On this cartoon by Arthur Young, child laborers are compared to medieval galley slaves.

AMERICAN CHILDREN   *The crew of a U. S. coal mine, about 1908.*

As late as 1864, a horrified Royal Commission was told the following by a Nottingham master sweep:

No one knows the cruelty a boy has to undergo in learning. The flesh must be hardened. This must be done by rubbing it, chiefly on the elbows and knees, with the strongest brine close by a hot fire. You must stand over them with a cane, or coax them by a promise of a halfpenny if they will stand a few more rubs. At first they will come back from their work streaming with blood, and the knees looking as if the caps had been pulled off. Then they must be rubbed with brine again.

In 1875, in a magisterial speech which created a deep impression, Lord Shaftesbury rebuked the whole country for being fully conscious of this horrible system for a hundred years and yet doing nothing about it, and for systematically disobeying those laws which had been passed by Parliament to deal with the abuses. Finally, the conscience of the English was aroused and Lord Shaftesbury brought the scandal to an end with the passage of his Chimney Sweepers Bill.

Although England had now passed some regulations concerning employment of children, the United States did not pass an effective Federal law controlling child labor until 1938.

An article in an 1830 issue of the *Mechanics' Free Press* described the situation in the Philadelphia cotton factories: children, six to seventeen, worked from daybreak to dark with a total of only one and a half hours allowed for three meals during the day.

In 1832, about two-fifths of all factory workers in New England were children. The first state-wide minimum age law, prohibiting the employment of children under 12 in textile mills, was passed in 1848 in Pennsylvania; but it was not until after

IS A BARGAIN ALWAYS CHEAP?   *A 1913 broadside raises the question.*

*THE ROMANCE OF CHILD
LABOR   British and American exploiters are attacked in this
1913 cartoon.*

CHILD LABOR   A 192
cartoon by Robert Minor.

AN ECONOMIC QUES-
TION   "Personally, I'm
opposed to child labor, but
Theodore says they're less
expensive." This cartoon
first appeared around 1935.

AUTOMATION   A mill owner visits a worker's wife. "Mrs. Crumb, I have called to assist you. We have just installed machinery that no longer necessitates your husband's services in the factory. These machines can be manipulated by three-year-old babies, and I am willing to give your child a chance."

GREEDY PARENTS   "One Reason for the Child Labor Problem" is the title of this 1903 American cartoon by W. A. Rogers.

VERMONT COTTON MILL *This girl, employed to walk up and down between the spinning frames and to knot any threads that broke, worked from six in the morning till six at night. For the regular 12 hours of work she earned $3 a week.*

APPEAL TO THE CHIEF EXECUTIVE *"Mr. President, we don't want anything. We just want to grow up," say the children in this cartoon, which appeared in 1913 in the old, now defunct "Life" magazine. During Wilson's first administration, reformers sought legislation to control child labor.*

NO TIME FOR TROUBLE
"See, it keeps them out of mischief," says the Senator, in a cartoon which appeared in the "New York World" in 1916. This argument was used by mill owners and powerful lobbies to oppose passage of child labor legislation then pending in Congress.

SOUTH CAROLINA
COTTON MILL

the Civil War that child labor became widely recognized as a problem in the U.S.

In 1870, some 750,000 children between the ages of 10 and 15—17% of all children that age—were engaged in full-time labor. Although many individual states enacted child labor laws during the next two decades, the number of working children continued to grow. The 1910 census showed that nearly two million children between the ages of 10 and 15 were employed in industry. Boys and girls, as young as eight, tended cotton looms; boys a year or two older stood all night before the furnaces in glass factories; lads of tender age worked as mule boys in coal mines. The average wage for youngsters in the glass industry was less than $3.00 a week. Almost one half of these children worked at least ten hours a day. In the clothing industry, the situation was possibly worse. Here the average wage for children was $2.00 a week.

As late as 1914, six Southern states had no law which made school attendance compulsory. Three times—in 1916, 1919, and again in 1933—Congress passed legislation regulating child labor, but all three laws were declared unconstitutional by the Supreme Court. In 1924, Congress drafted a constitutional amendment that gave the Federal Government the power to regulate the labor of persons under 18. By 1937, however, only 28 states had ratified the amendment. Efforts to secure its passage were halted.

Finally, in 1938, Congress passed the Fair Labor Standards Act, which established 16 as the minimum age for work during school hours in industries involved in interstate commerce. A minimum age of 18 was ordained for specified hazardous occupations. Children of 14 could be employed after school hours in non-mining and non-manufacturing occupations.

As recently as 1957, the National Child Labor committee reported that in California a migrant fruit picker was badly hurt in a collision while being transported in a truck. The boy

CHILD LABOR TODAY   *This young agricultural worker is one among millions who, even today, labor in field, workshop, and domestic service, instead of going to school. In the less developed countries of the world, countless children work for meager wages, prematurely exhausting their strength and growing up without education.*

was only 11 years old; he had been working 54 hours a week!

Even today, when all 50 states have laws regulating child labor, children of agricultural migrant workers still work eight hours a day and longer. The number of working childen has greatly diminished, but the scandal of child labor still remains.

HENRY VIII AND HIS SIX WIVES

No English king in history treated his consorts worse than Henry VIII. Though he may have been a good judge of women, he was a poor judge of queens. Two of his wives, Anne Boleyn and Catherine Howard, behaved so impulsively that Henry resorted to the headsman to end their royal careers.

Oceans of tears were shed in subsequent centuries over Anne Boleyn and Catherine Howard. But England in Henry's day wept for neither. Anne Boleyn was dismissed as a "goggle-eyed whore" who was justly punished; Catherine Howard was considered a flighty piece whose past caught up with her. Each was a commoner, related to the ambitious and cordially detested Norfolk family, and neither had inherited a royal birthright. For their queens the English preferred the daughters of princes.

Henry VIII had six wives and queens, but his subjects recognized only one true queen—his first, Catherine of Aragon. It was his treatment of her which so affronted his people and his world.

Many historians have dealt harshly with Henry. People have considered him a wife-killer, a lustful sadist and other unsavory things. Yet, during his thirty-eight year reign he was enormously popular. His people loved and admired him. The brunt of the years of terror which he instituted between 1534 and 1540, and which has blackened his name in history books,

was supported only by the relatively few aristocrats who opposed him. The people, on the other hand, retained a freedom
remarkable for the times, commenting with the utmost candor
on the King's affairs.

Their angry reaction to the trial and divorce of Catherine of
Aragon caused Henry the greatest concern. He felt he had
outraged the conscience of his people.

Catherine of Aragon was the daughter of King Ferdinand
of Aragon and Queen Isabella of Castile, two capable monarchs who had welded Spain into a single kingdom and laid
the foundations of its greatness.

*HENRY VIII   This portrait by Holbein captures Henry's strength and stub-
bornness, and also conveys the splendor of his court.*

*Of Henry's six wives, be beheaded two, divorced two, and lost one in child-
birth. Only the sixth survived him. His several marriages had the sanction of his
highly appointed ecclesiastics, but were not recognized by the Pope.*

*Wavering between their allegiances, the clergy of England could only guess
which side—the Protestants or the Catholics—would triumph. Some supported
Henry's Protestantism through his reign and through the short rule of his son,
Edward VI, who succeeded him. Many of these same Protestants were later
martyred in the purges of "Bloody Mary," the Catholic daughter of Henry and
Catherine of Aragon, the queen who followed Edward VI to the throne. Under
her successor, the Protestant Elizabeth I, those who embraced Mary's Catholicism now found themselves once again on the wrong side of the fence. "Good
Queen Bess," as she later came to be known, was Henry the VIII's daughter by
Anne Boleyn, and she led England into the golden Elizabethan Age of prosperity and culture.*

· NO · ETATIS · · SVÆ · XLIX

CATHERINE OF ARAGON   Henry's loyal wife for eighteen years, she was divorced arbitrarily, through long and controversial proceedings, which led to Henry's break with the Catholic Church, and the consequent establishment of the Church of England.

In 1501 the Infanta Dona Catalina arrived in England to marry Prince Arthur, the eldest son of Henry VII and heir to the throne. As with most alliances of state in the sixteenth century this marriage had resulted from prolonged and often venal bargaining between the respective parents. Ferdinand and Isabella wanted their daughter to be Queen of England and permanent ambassadress to London. Henry VII encouraged the match mainly for financial reasons. Catherine would bring a huge dowry.

She was sixteen. She created a striking and lasting impression on the English. She had lovely long auburn hair which added to her singular beauty. She had a lively, intelligent face, lovely manners and a regal demeanor. England took her to its collective heart and never ceased to love her.

She was married immediately to Arthur Prince of Wales, a sickly youth whose physique compared badly with that of his strapping young brother, Prince Henry.

It was said that Arthur, a boy of sixteen, was not physically able to consummate the marriage. In less than six months the youthful bridegroom was in his grave. Both Catherine and her ladies-in-waiting declared to the end that he had never been her lover.

But Arthur, apparently, boasted otherwise, and he may have been telling the truth; although there seems to have been little attraction between the two young people· They could not speak each other's language and had to resort to a painful Latin.

The consummation or non-consummation of this marriage became a vital issue in later years. It led indirectly to Henry VIII's break with Rome, the Reformation, and the establishment of the Protestant Church in England.

In those days royal wedding nights were scarcely private affairs. In some European countries officials noted all that happened in the nuptial chamber, even recording for posterity the number of times the royal pair performed the marital act. Anxiety about the royal line, rather than prurience, countenanced this watchful eye upon the royal bed.

Whatever happened on that wedding night in 1501 and on the nights which followed, the matter was to have far-reaching and tragic consequences for Catherine.

With Arthur dead, Henry VII did not wish to lose Catherine's huge dowry, only half of which had been paid. He tastelessly proposed that he himself should marry the girl-widow, but her parents conceived another way of fulfilling their daughter's planned destiny. She would marry Prince Henry, now heir to the throne.

ANNE BOLEYN   This lovely, headstrong commoner married Henry VIII in 1533, shortly before the birth of their daughter Elizabeth. Both Anne and her sister had reportedly been mistresses of the King. Her elevation to the throne was extremely unpopular, not only with the Catholic Church, but also with the general populace. Anne's royal alliance was short-lived, as Henry soon had her beheaded for adultery.

ANNA BOLINA VXOR— ⋯ HENRI· OCTA

JANE SEYMOUR Henry's third wife, a former lady-in-waiting, bore him his only male heir, Edward VI. Twelve days after Edward's birth, Jane died.

Isabella of Spain was not named "the Catholic" without reason. Her influence in Rome was enormous, and the alledgely unconsummated marriage between Catherine and Arthur was quickly annulled by the Pope.

Prince Henry and Catherine were married amidst criticism and suspicion. Many ecclesiastical authorities in England believed the marriage incestuous, violating the biblical injunction that a man must not marry his brother's wife.

Unpredictably, the marriage was in many ways successful. Henry, now king, and Catherine, now queen, were happy for years. Younger than his wife, he was a husband she delighted in. Taller, stronger, more brilliant, more witty, more learned and more cultured than almost anyone in his kingdom, Henry was a magnificent extrovert, a fine glittering figure of a king.

Catherine, herself intelligent and accomplished, blossomed into a woman of sweetness and charm. Her fascinating Spanish accent continued to lend enchantment to her most ordinary speech. Of royal birth herself, Catherine even knew when to turn a blind eye to her husband's occasional infidelities.

Except for one drawback, which led to national consequences so tremendous that Henry could not ignore them, theirs would have been one of the most felicitous royal marriages in history. After eighteen years, Catherine had given birth to eight children, but only one, Princess Mary, had survived infancy.

Henry believed he desperately needed a male heir. The Tudor line was insecure. His father had had only a precarious title to the throne, though he had been one of the most successful English monarchs in centuries. Henry VIII was well aware of his historically insecure position. He believed that if there was no male heir to succeed him, his death would precipitate civil war. Catherine's child bearing days drew to a close, and Henry faced the bitter prospect of a sonless future. He may have overestimated the seriousness of this problem but his feelings were understandable. England had never had a queen regnant, and many believed it constitutionally impossible for a woman to ascend the throne. Henry could not foresee the reign of both his daughters, Mary and Elizabeth, and he could civil war. Catherine's child-bearing days drew to a close, and not foresee that Elizabeth's reign would be more glorious than his own.

The fact that he, handsome and virile as he was, had no legitimate issue (though he did have an illegitimate son) was both a sorrow and a shame. He began to believe that God was punishing him for having married his brother's widow.

He attempted to arrange a marriage between Princess Mary and the Emperor Charles V, so that their son would be emperor on the Continent as well as king of England—a glittering dynastic prospect for the Tudors. But the proposed alliance did not go through. Charles' refusal was partly due to his doubts of the validity of Henry's marriage, and therefore of Mary's legitimacy; an issue which had long been debated in European theological circles.

ANNE OF CLEVES   The daughter of a German duke, Anne did not particularly want to marry Henry VIII. The marital arrangements were made in 1540. After six months, she maneuvered him into a divorce.

Henry was left with his problem, and he faced it with the naive cruelty of his age.

He told Catherine—already desperately unhappy and oppressed by her failure to produce a male heir—that their marriage had not been legal, that for eighteen years they had lived in sin, and that the early deaths of all their male children had been the punishment of God. Her duty, he told her, was to go into religious retreat.

Catherine uttered no word of protest or argument. She broke down and wept. She confused and confounded him by a flood of desolate tears. She knew well enough that her cause was hopeless. Still, after the first shock, she was determined not to give in without a fight.

She knew, as did everyone else, of Anne Boleyn. Anne was dark-eyed, intelligent, curiously attractive, and she played her cards cleverly. Anne was determined to supplant the middle-aged Catherine, and Henry was determined to have her succeed.

In the struggle Anne had every advantage, including youth. She was twenty, Henry thirty-six, Catherine forty. Henry intended that Anne should bear him the Prince of Wales who would one day succeed him.

CATHERINE HOWARD   The niece of the Duke of Norfolk, Catherine survived for two years as Henry's fifth wife. Then he had her beheaded.

ETATIS   SVÆ ·21·

Both he and Catherine sincerely believed they were cursed: Catherine, because her marriage to Arthur many years before had been sealed by the blood of the young Earl of Warwick; Henry, because he believed he was suffering the penalty of the ancient Levitical law for taking his brother's wife. Many of his contemporaries shared in his conviction of sin as sincerely as he. How else could the death of Catherine's many children be explained?

When the people heard that Henry was thinking of putting aside his wife of eighteen years, they were scandalized. They thought he was mad. They knew Catherine as a virtuous woman; in their eyes Anne Boleyn was a whore. Why would God give the whore a prince when He had denied one to the good Queen Catherine?

CATHERINE PARR   In 1543, Henry married his sixth wife who proceeded to outlive him. Though she bore no children, she became a powerful Dowager Queen with great influence over Henry's three children—Mary, Elizabeth, and Edward VI.

They were outraged at the thought that the whole panoply of papal authority should be invoked to destroy the marriage of King Henry and the highborn Spanish princess just to enthrone the despised Anne Boleyn, a commoner. And had not her sister also been the king's mistress?

But the Pope's reluctance to dissolve the marriage was not due to these considerations. Pope Clement VII* was completely in the power of Charles V, whose armies had overrun Italy. Since Charles was Catherine's nephew, the Pope knew what his attitude should be. He steadfastly refused to break the marriage of the King of England. When, under great pressure, he finally agreed to let the case be tried in England, he secretly instructed the court to adjourn without pronouncing judgment.

The trial began on May 29, 1529, in the Great Hall of Blackfriars. Much to Henry's anger and disappointment, the people were obviously behind Queen Catherine. No arguments could shake their indignation at the shameful way their King was putting aside his loyal consort. They were not even greatly concerned about England's need for a Tudor heir.

The Pope had appointed Cardinal Wolsey and Cardinal Campeggio, an Italian, as legates to hear the case. They were supported by all the English bishops. On a raised dais were special chairs for the King and Queen, but they rarely attended the deliberately protracted proceedings.

On only one day, June 21, were Catherine and Henry together in court. It was a memorable occasion.

Henry had told the court of his resolve to no longer live in sin with his consort. His conscience was troubled. The court

---

* Not to be confused with the Clement VII who reigned at Avignon from 1378 to 1394 and who was later declared anti-Pope. His style of Clement VII being expunged, the next Clement was free to take it. In the same way there are two Popes with the style John XXIII—the notorious one who was deposed by the Council of Constance in 1415, and the modern pontiff now counted as one of the greatest of the Popes.

must speedily decide on the legality of his marriage to Queen Catherine.

All eyes turned to Catherine for her reply. Instead of addressing the court, she walked over the King's chair. She knelt at his feet and said:

> *Sire, I beseech you, for all the love that hath been between us, and for the love of God, let me have justice and right, take of me some pity and compunction, for I am a poor woman and a stranger born out of your dominion. I have here no assured friend, and much less indifferent counsel. I flee to you, as to the head of justice within this realm.*
>
> *I take God, and all this world, to witness that I have been to you a true, humble and obedient wife, ever conformable to your will and pleasure. I loved all those you loved, only for your sake, whether they were my friends or mine enemies. This twenty years I have been your true wife, and by me ye have had divers children, although it hath pleased God to call them out of this world, which has been no fault of mine.*
>
> *And when ye had me at the first, I take God to be my judge I was a true maid without touch of man, and whether it be true or no I put it to your conscience. To God I commit my cause.*

Henry found himself moved. He was prepared for argument, indignation, even anger. But this dignified, loyal and reproachful speech put him to shame. In silence, he watched her make a low obeisance and then leave the court. Although she was recalled, she refused to return to a place where she knew there was no justice.

"My lords," said King Henry to the murmuring conclave of

churchmen, "she is as true, as obedient, and as conformable a wife as I could in my fantasy wish or desire· She has all the virtuous qualities that ought to be in a woman of her dignity, or in any other of baser estate."

All the same, he presented his case to the court: that she was not a virgin when she came to his bed.

Witnesses testified that Catherine's boy bridegroom, Prince Arthur, had stated: "I have tonight been in the middle of Spain." Their memory of a chance remark made by the heir to the throne twenty-eight years before, is perhaps unconvincing. On the other hand, Arthur would undoubtedly have wanted to consummate his marriage, presuming his capability to do so; a capability which history, on slender evidence, has consistently doubted. In the sixteenth century, a prince was a man at fifteen and was expected to behave like a man.

On the other hand, Catherine swore to her dying day that her first marriage was never consummated. A deeply religious woman, she gave her oath in the confessional that she had been a virgin when she married Henry. Henry swore the contrary. History has chosen to believe Catherine.

Certainly the citizens of London believed her and were passionately on her side. When she came out of the court on that June day of 1529, she stepped out to cheering crowds.

There was no published report of the trial. Yet the people

MARRIAGE TRIAL   In the presence of the canonical court appointed to rule on the validity of their marriage, Catherine of Aragon pleads with her husband for justice.

were kept well informed of the proceedings in the Great Hall of Blackfriars. They did not like what they heard, and they expressed their opinions plainly.

Henry, who valued the good will of his people, and whose power rested on the carefully won support of both the people and Parliament, was in a black mood. Anne Boleyn hardly dared show her face in court.

Now Henry called a representative meeting in London and explained his case in person.

When the legative court assembled before Henry to pronounce its verdict on the legality of the royal marriage it did nothing more than adjourn, shelving the decision in accordance with its secret instructions from Rome.

In a deadly silence Henry rose and stalked out of the hall. This was the turning point of his reign. This moment marked the end of many things: the career of Wolsey; papal authority in England; even the English mediaeval system.

CHARLES V, HOLY ROMAN EMPEROR   *Nephew of Catherine of Aragon, Charles V, the greatest of all the Hapsburgs, loomed as a constant threat and a check upon Henry VIII. War with Charles might easily have broken out over religion, over Catherine's honor, or over more minor considerations, and Charles would have to be reckoned with as a formidable opponent.*

Charles had inherited an empire on which the sun never set. His territories included the Spanish kingdoms, Spanish America, Naples, Sicily, the Low Countries, and much of Germany and Austria. When he conquered Mexico and Peru, Charles brought the Spanish-dominated period of the Holy Roman Empire to its height.

THOMAS WOLSEY Cardinal
and Archbishop of York &c.

H. Holbein Pinxit.   R. Sheppard Sculp.

THOMAS WOLSEY   The cardinal and statesman, as lord chancellor and then papal legate, dominated the English political scene throughout the first twenty years of Henry VIII's reign. Wolsey was a man of prodigious energy, quick mind, tenacious memory, remarkable capacity for detail, intense self-confidence, and optimism. As early as 1509 he held a place in the royal council where he gained great influence over the young Henry. Henry, by nature often erratic and indolent, entrusted more and more of his cares and duties to Wolsey.

In 1515, Wolsey received two high appointments: he was created cardinal by Pope Leo X, and also chosen lord chancellor of England. He entered a thirteen-year period of almost unlimited power in foreign and domestic, clerical and secular affairs.

In foreign policy, Wolsey attempted to become the arbiter of Europe. He believed that if a near-balance were maintained between France and the Holy Roman Empire, England could control matters by merely threatening to take sides.

In domestic matters, Wolsey proved himself to be a great jurist, and exercised powerful influence over the developing judicial system in England.

In clerical affairs, he instituted some monastic reforms and made many commendable church appointments. Nevertheless, he was guilty of some abuses of his power: he held several lucrative sees simultaneously, and he lavished preferments on his illegitimate son, Thomas Winter.

Through the years, he made many enemies. Some were merely jealous of his power; some had sinister motives.

Wolsey fell from power in 1529. Three reasons are seen for his dramatic crash: (1) He failed to acquire for Henry VIII a church divorce from Catherine of Aragon. (2) He had failed in an attempt to take over complete administration of the English church. (3) His foreign policy had so miscarried that England was virtually isolated and endangered from all sides. His enemies, who included Anne Boleyn's father and uncle, seized upon his failure to formalize the royal divorce in July, 1529. In October of that year, he was stripped of his offices. In an attempt to regain some power, he entered into plans and correspondence; but in November, 1530, he was arrested. A sick and humbled man, he died that same month, while traveling to London to face his king.

It marked the end, too, of poor Catherine of Aragon, perhaps England's most scandalously ill-used queen. Unlike most of Henry's victims she had done nothing to deserve her fate.

Henry stormed to Parliament and demanded there what the papal court would not give him. Parliament did not deny him his wish. Henry informed the Pope that he, the King, was now Head of the English Church.

The Vatican reacted with horror and anger. The Pope forbade Henry to proceed with a second marriage or to cohabit with any woman save Queen Catherine, on pain of excommunication. The Pope in fact issued a further edict forbidding all women to marry King Henry VIII of England.

England, on a tide of anticlericalism and antipopery, stood by their king. Catherine's individual wrongs were nearly forgotten in a wave of outraged nationalism.

Nevertheless, Henry did not have his own way. His proposed marriage to the arrogant and hated Anne Boleyn was extremely unpopular. His people still regarded him as a man trying to get rid of his faithful wife in order to marry his mistress.

Many people feared that the Emperor Charles V would take up arms to defend his ill-used aunt. Members of Parliament publicly begged Henry to solve his matrimonial problems by taking back his queen. Henry was enraged by all this criticism, although, unlike some of his unwise descendants on the throne, he never opposed Parliament. He was far too clever. His strength lay in the fact that he never acted outside the law.

Anne was now pregnant. The marriage must be hastened to legitimize the expected prince. It took place secretly in January, 1533, assisted by Archbishop Cranmer, who pronounced the marriage to Catherine invalid. The baby arrived —a girl. Henry was bitterly disappointed. He need not have been, for the child became Elizabeth I, the "Good Queen

Bess" of England's great age of prosperity.

As people do, Englishmen became reconciled to a *fait accompli*.

Meanwhile, Catherine returned to seclusion, and was parted from her beloved daughter Mary. Even in her unhappy obscurity she was not left in peace; she was ordered to swear that Anne Boleyn was now queen and Henry's lawful wife, and that Mary was a bastard. This she passionately refused to do.

But she was ill and not far from her end. From her death-bed, in 1536, she sent a letter to Henry which moved him to tears.

Beginning "My lord and dear husband," she forgave him for the wrong he had done her, and she prayed that God would pardon him. She concluded with these remarkable and revealing words: "Lastly do I vow that my eyes desire you above all things."

Henry could weep and overlook the pathetic, obstinate signature under the letter—"Catherine Queen of England"; nevertheless his relief was great when she finally died. Her death lifted from England the fear of war with Charles V.

Catherine's death marked the end of one great scandal, and the beginning of a series of murders by the royal bluebeard which is unparalleled in English history.

THE FRENCH GALLEY SLAVES

Then he showed us how he commanded their motions with a nod and his whistle, making them row out. This was to me the newest spectacle I could imagine . . . beholding so many hundreds of miserably naked persons, having their heads shaven close, wearing red bonnets and a pair of coarse canvas drawers only, with their whole back and legs stark naked, and doubly chained about their middle and legs in couples, and made fast to their seats: they were all commanded by an imperious and cruel seaman, to whom they gave instant obedience. . . . Their rising forwards, and falling back at their oar, is a miserable spectacle; and the noise of their chains and the roaring of the beaten waters has something of the strange and fearful in it. They are ruled and chastised by the whip upon their backs and the soles of their feet at the least disorder and without the least humanity.

This quaint, grim paragraph was written by John Evelyn, an English diarist, in 1644. Evelyn set down his impressions after being sumptuously entertained by the commander of the French *Galley Royale*. The captain's cabin was the last word in 17th-century luxury, and music was played while his party dined.

Ancre

Organeau Anneau de fer autour
duquel on roule un Cable

Trou de l'Ancre ou passe l'Organeau

Bout de la Verque ou
l'on met le Jas.

Verge ou Verque

Patte   Patte
Oreille Bras Bras Oreille
Croisée de
l'Ancre

Jas ou Essieu ou Jouet de l'Ancre.

Ancre

Organeau Anneau de fer

Jas ou   Essieu

Verge ou Verque

Patte   Patte
Oreille   Oreille ou laronie
de la Patte
Croisée de
l'Ancre

F

M

E

C

B

A

T

FRENCH GALLEY   *This drawing of the French ship "La Reale" shows the vessel's design and also some of the hundreds of slaves that were required to propel it.*

UNDER THE LASH   In a Turkish galley, slaves are chained five or six to an oar. The boatswain walks up and down a gangplank, wielding his terrible lash.

In the eighteenth century, conditions in French galleys were surprisingly similar to those in the supposedly more barbaric non-Christian countries farther east.

In addition to the *Galley Royale*, there were 25 other galleys in port at Marseilles. Each of these was manned by up to 200 slaves—*galeriens* they were called by their French overseers. Branded upon the back of each slave with a hot iron were the letters GAL. These would be with them until death.

By 1644, when Evelyn visited Marseilles, the galley slave had a 2,000-year history behind him. Even before the days of ancient Greece and Rome, felons and prisoners-of-war were made to propel these awkward ships upon the calm

waters of the Mediterranean, bleeding and dying under intolerable labor, foul food, and the whip of the overseer.

By the Middle Ages, it had become customary to sentence
condemned felons to the galleys. In 1564, Charles IX of
France decreed that the minimum term a prisoner should serve
as a galley slave was 10 years. Only if he were wounded in
combat, could a convict be granted his freedom earlier.

The temper of the 17th-century was unbelievably cruel.
Those deemed wicked were to be given a foretaste of
hell—the hell of a Dante with sadisms inconceivable. The

GREEK TRIREME   In this bas relief from the Acropolis Museum in Athens only the top layer of oarsmen are visible above shipside. Twice as many more are laboring in the hull.

ANCIENT EGYPTIAN SHIPS A slightly more primitive form of galley is seen in this drawing of an ancient Egyptian boat. The Theban vessel is shown returning richly laden from a voyage to Arabia.

galley bench was the nearest thing to that hell that human ingenunity could devise.

The galley slave had few historians to record the miseries of his long death-in-life. Not until Jean Marteilhe.

Marteilhe was a French Huguenot, who served 12 years in the galleys—not for being a criminal—but because of his religious beliefs. His autobiography, *Memoirs of a Protestant,* published in 1758 in England, remains the classic authority on what it was like to be a galley slave.

Jean Marteilhe had the misfortune to be born in 1684 in Bergerac, 60 miles east of Bordeaux on the River Dordogne. One year later, Louis XIV, France's "Sun King," revoked the Edict of Nantes, a step which made life almost unbearable for his Protestant subjects. Marteilhe and his family were Protestants, as were most of the inhabitants of Bergerac, and his childhood was spent under the stifling terror of King Louis XIV's anti-Huguenot campaign.

When Jean Marteilhe was 16 years old, in October of 1700, one of the severest forms of persecution befell the Marteilhe family. Twenty-two dragoons were assigned to be quartered in the Marteilhe home. These soldiers—execrable men noted for their cruelty and ignorance—were widely feared throughout France. The quartering of such troops in a Huguenot household was a standard terroist tactic. As if the imposition of the dragoons were not enough, Marteilhe's father was put in prison. His younger brothers were sent to a convent to be educated as Catholics. After suffering "the most horrible tortures," Madame Marteilhe was forced to sign an abjuration of her Protestant faith.

Just before the dragoons entered his house, Jean Marteilhe managed to escape. He fled Bergerac by night, avoiding the sentries. With a young friend, Daniel le Gras, he hoped to escape to Calvinist Holland.

The two boys got as far as the Netherlands frontier before they were caught. In jail, a number of attempts were made to persuade them to forsake their religion. But although the curate used every wile—including, Marteilhe tells us, the offer of his young and beautiful niece complete with a fat dowry— Marteilhe and Le Gras stood steadfast. Hauled before the judge at Tournai, the two were condemned to the galleys for life. All of their property—which consisted only of the clothes on their backs—was confiscated.

Pilate fashion, the judge washed his hands of the cruel sentence. "It is the King's order which condemns you," he told them.

Citizens of Tournai mounted a petition on the boys' behalf. Since the signers put their lives and their liberty into jeopardy, this act was evidence of overwhelming sympathy. But the petition was arrogantly rejected by the Minister of State.

"Jean Marteilhe and Daniel le Gras, having been found upon the frontiers without passports, His Majesty decides that they shall be condemned to the galleys."

The two were fettered and taken to Lille, where other galley slaves had been collected. From there, they were marched to Dunkirk. At Dunkirk, they were chained to the rowing benches of a galley named ironically *L'Heureuse*—Happiness.

A good deal larger than the standard war galley of those days, *L'Heureuse* was 150 feet long, and floated so low in the water that she was frequently awash. When fully manned she was so crowded that no one, not even the officers, could

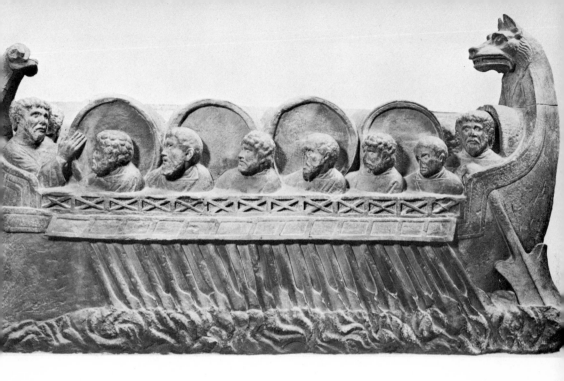

SLAVE SHIPS   *In the Roman boat above, to simplify his design, the sculptor omitted about 16 of the men needed to handle the oars. In art, the galley slave's work might look graceful; in real life, it was totally wretched.*

   Below is the design of an ancient Greek five-banked galley, called a quinquireme.

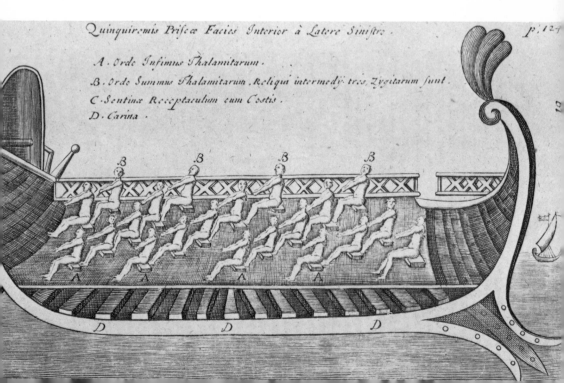

Quinquiremis Priscæ Facies Interior à Latere Sinistro.   *p. 124*

A. Ordo Infimus Thalamitarum.
B. Ordo Summus Thalamitarum. Reliqui intermedij tres Zygitarum sunt.
C. Sentinæ Receptaculum cum Costis.
D. Carina.

HUGUENOT REVOLUTION FAILS After the ill-fated "Conspiracy of Am-
boise" in 1560 in which French Protestants attempted to seize control of the
government, the captured Huguenot revolutionists are executed. This revolt and

subsequent executions were only brief incidents in the long, bitter struggle between Catholics and Protestants that wracked Europe during the 16th and 17th Centuries.

stretch out to full length. The full complement of *L'Heureuse* consisted of 10 officers, 25 sailors, and no fewer than 300 slave rowers. The oars were over 50 feet long, 13 feet of them inboard, very heavily weighted to balance their outboard length. Wooden handles were riveted to the oars, since the oars themselves were too large to grasp. Each rower was assigned to one pair of handles.

The benches upon which they slaved, slept when allowed to, and ate when they were fed, were six-inch-wide beams, set only four feet apart. These benches were padded with wool and old sacking. It was to these boards the slaves were chained.

To row, a man had first to thrust out the huge handle of his oar over the bodies of those in front of him. Then he stood to let the blade strike the water; and then, on command, he threw himself violently backwards. The bench was padded to lessen the jar as the stroke was completed.

The *galerien's* back was bare. His efforts were directed by drivers or *comites,* stationed on the center gangway. Their long hide whips sang out upon the back of any slave who showed the slightest sign of weariness.

Only the kiss of the whip on his naked flesh made it possible for any slave to sustain such a frightful and prolonged effort. Marteilhe reports that he often rowed full force for 24 hours without rest. During such periods of extreme agony, the *comites* and petty officers would walk along the rowing benches putting wine-soaked biscuits into the mouths of the rowers, to sustain them from fainting. When a slave did faint at the oar, he was flogged back to consciousness. When he died of semi-starvation, pain, and exhaustion, he was flung into the sea. And not a beat was missed.

The drivers were sadistic brutes who had been apprenticed to their ugly trade from boyhood. Marteilhe bore them no ill-will. If they did not flog the rowers hard enough, they, in

JOHN EVELYN   *The English diarist reported his visit in 1644 aboard the "Galley Royale" in Marseilles. While the overseer whipped the chained, hard-laboring oarsmen, Evelyn and his party were sumptuously wined and dined.*

ROMAN GALLEY   *An accurately restored model of an ancient Roman trieme—*
a ship with three banks of oars. The required three rows of oarsmen sat in the dark,
dank hull of the ship. In the event of a shipwreck or a military disaster, their location
and their chains generally prevented them from escaping.

LOUIS XIV OF FRANCE   *Because he feared the Protestant minority as a*
threat to his country's unity, Louis XIV oppressed them harshly. Although his
court was highly refined and civilized in other respects, Louis perpetuated and
even encouraged the barbaric tradition of the galleys. This portrait is by Hyacin-
the Rigaud.

turn, were abused by their superior officer. It was those officers, supposedly educated men, whom Marteilhe could not
forgive. The captain of *L'Heureuse,* whose name was De la
Pailleterie, disliked the Huguenot slaves much more than he
did the thugs and murderers chained to the oars of his galley.
Aboard *L'Heureuse* to be a Protestant was almost a death
warrent.

Marteilhe, a good-looking boy of 17, was fortunate enough
to escape a good deal of the suffering inflicted upon his com-

HUGUENOT REFUGEES Dispossessed by the revocation of the Edict of Nantes in 1685, crowds of French Protestant emigres arrive at Dover.

panions. One of the drivers took a fancy to him, and Marteilhe's back, more often than not, escaped the lash. This particular *comite* was not without a spark of humanity. He seemed to understand that Marteilhe was no criminal.

Although the officers hated the Huguenots, they were treated with some deference by the *comites* and by the ordinary convicts, who addressed them as "sir," and who took the view that if the Huguenots were damned for their religion, they would undergo sufficient punishment in the world to

ST. BARTHOLOMEW'S DAY MASSACRE *In 1572, when the Calvinist Admiral Coligny attempted to arrange French aid for the Protestant Netherlands against Catholic Spain, leading French Catholics panicked and took drastic action. On August 24, St. Batholomew's Day, the bloody work began. At the instiga-*

tion of Catherine de' Medici, mother of the young French King Charles IX, Coligny and thousands of his fellow Protestants were killed. The victims probably· numbered 8,000 in Paris alone, and another 20,000 throughout France.

come without being tortured to death in this one.

Marteilhe survived seven years of hellish existence. Finally, he was wounded in a battle in the Thames estuary, and lost the use of his arm. But the rule that a slave wounded in the service of France should automatically gain his freedom did not apply to Protestants. However, Marteilhe somehow managed to become secretary to the commodore.

In the meantime, Louis XIV was defeated in the war of the Spanish succession. One of the stipulations of the ensuing Peace of Utrecht was that the English would occupy the city of Dunkirk until it was demilitarized. When the triumphant soldiers of the English garrison arrived, they flocked to the galleys, embraced the galley slaves, and demanded their immediate release.

The Catholic churchmen of Dunkirk were both frightened and embarrassed by the situation. In vain they tried to prevent anyone from going near the galleys. Irrational in their hatred, the Catholics were determined that the Huguenots should not be freed, and they proceeded, one night, to smuggle their Protestant prisoners out of Dunkirk, transporting them by sea to Calais. There the galley slaves were chained once again—Jean Marteilhe among them—and marched across France. Some reached the galleys in Marseilles, but many died along the way. Marteilhe, who seemed able to endure almost anything, survived this death march, too.

In Marseilles there were 40 galleys in port. Once again Marteilhe was chained to the rowing benches.

The English were now in full cry, vociferously demanding the release of the galley slaves. The French Catholic priests were clearly desperate, and swarmed aboard the galleys, working among the obdurate Huguenots, trying to convert them to the true faith.

Meanwhile, at Versailles, Louis was under pressure by the Catholic hierarchy not to permit the release of the slaves. The missionary efforts at Marseilles, he was assured, were being undertaken on his behalf, to save face for the King of France. If these efforts succeeded, it could then be said that the heretics had returned to the true faith of their own free will, and that intercession by the heretical English Queen was quite uncalled for.

However, the slaves resisted conversion; and towards the end of 1713, the English brought such pressure to bear on the Sun King that proud Louis was compelled to order the release of all Protestant slaves in his royal galleys. The *galeriens* were ordered to leave the king's realm at their own expense.

A kindly captain offered passage to the released Huguenots. Yet even up to the last moment, the frustrated priests still tried to delay the departure of the galley slaves.

Eventually, Marteilhe made his way to London by way of Piedmont, Geneva, and Cologne. In London, he and 12 other liberated Huguenots were presented to Queen Anne, whose hand they kissed in heartfelt gratitude. Even the French ambassador congratulated them upon their release.

Marteilhe seemed to bear no ill will against his native country, nor even towards Louis XIV who had been responsible for subjecting him to 12 years of savage torment. Marteilhe's attitude remains a notable example of Christian forbearance. Of Daniel le Gras, his companion in servitude, Marteilhe says nothing. The inference is that Le Gras died.

Marteilhe's book, which appeared in Rotterdam in 1757, was published in London the following year, and became a powerful piece of propaganda. Marteilhe's writings did much to shame and discredit the French Catholicism of that century.

VAN MEEGEREN: MASTER FORGER

Han van Meegeren is one of the few art forgers in history who was also a great painter. This brilliant Dutch artist holds the unique distinction of having made fools of more recognized art critics and European experts than any other known hoaxer. His story is both exhilarating and pathetic. The fact that his masterfull forgeries may well be worth a fortune in their own right is his only and final reply to those who hounded him to prison and to death.

His story begins in The Hague, in 1927. At the age of thirty-eight, van Meegeren was still scratching out a living as an unsuccessful painter. Although he borrowed from the Impressionists and post-Impressionists, in his heart van Meegeren was not an artist in the modern tradition. The concepts of the avant-garde left him untouched, and their success only served to increase his smouldering resentment at his own failure to win overwhelming artistic recognition. Had he lived three hundred years before, he might well have been a pupil of Jan Vermeer (also known as Jan van der Meer van Delft), whose work he greatly admired and whose style became, in a sense, his own.

Vermeer had been forgotten for a couple of centuries after his death. Many of his pictures had been sold under the names of more popular Dutch artists such as de Hooch, Metsu, Ter Borch and even Rembrandt. A Frenchman named Thoré rediscovered him in the nineteenth century. Vermeer's paintings

have color, style, and a bold simplicity; some of them more
than hold their own beside Rembrandt. Vermeer, in fact, now
ranks with Rembrandt as a Dutch national hero. His paintings
are as revered and studied in Holland as Shakespeare's plays
are in England.

After making an intensive study of Vermeer, van Meegeren
found he was able to imitate his style with remarkable ease
and virtuosity. A dealer looking at one of his Vermeer copies
in his studio told him that if he had not known that van Meegeren had painted it, he would have said it was a genuine
Vermeer worth a million pounds. He should never have
opened his mouth, for it was soon after this experience that
van Meegeren conceived the idea of his magnificent fraud.
There were relatively few authentic Vermeers. Both the circumstances of Vermeer's life and his eclipse after his death
made it probable that there were unknown Vermeers in the
world waiting to be discovered. Van Meegeren proposed to
paint one himself, convinced that he alone had the talent to do
so. The spirit of the master, he felt, had certainly descended
upon him.

In 1932 he left Holland with his wife and went to live on the
Riviera where he produced his first "Vermeer." He began his
experiment by spending months in studying and exploring the
techniques used by Vermeer, his methods and materials, the
specific kinds of paint, brushes, and canvas. Vermeer used
brushes of bodger's hair, and these van Meegeren obtained.
He purchased old canvases of the Vermeer period and cleaned
off every fragment of the original paint. At last he felt that
he had mastered the technique; he had the materials; and he
never doubted his ability to paint the picture. One great
problem remained.

The paint on a picture three hundred years old possesses a
hardness which modern paintings naturally lack. How to
harden the paint was a problem that took him a long time to

solve. He finally solved it by baking the finished canvas in a precisely heated oven.

But van Meegeren was much more than a forger. He was not *copying* a Vermeer. He was *painting* an entirely new picture in the artist's style, which he hoped would be taken for a hitherto unknown Vermeer. He even went beyond that. He proposed to develop a "middle period" for the master—one that he could continue to exploit. Van Meegeren would create non-existent masterpieces. It was a bold stroke of imagination; but then, he himself was an artist of great merit.

It took him four years of concentrated work and study to complete his first Vermeer—"Christ at Emmaus"—a splendidly grouped picture of four figures around a table, with Christ breaking the bread.

Van Meegeren took his painting to Amsterdam in 1937, and showed it to an art expert. He explained his possession of the painting most plausibly. He said that, though he was an artist by profession, he had always done a certain amount of buying and selling of pictures. In France he had been in touch with a certain noble family, in financial straits, anxious to dispose of some old paintings. He found the Vermeer hidden in a corner of their attic. There was no reason to doubt van Meegeren's story. Many priceless canvases have been discovered in just such a way. After an examination of the picture, the expert was quite satisfied that it was a genuine Vermeer.

In due time, it was exhibited at Boymans Museum, and all the leading art critics and experts of Holland gathered at a private viewing to appraise this magnificent new find.

All were agreed that only Vermeer could have painted such a masterpiece. Everything about it: the quality of the paint; the solidity of the figures; the balance of the composition; all betrayed the hand of the master. Everyone agreed, too, that it was painted during Vermeer's middle period, about 1660. It

HAN VAN MEEGEREN The great Dutch art forger stands before a painting.

was, of course, signed by Vermeer in what was technically described as "the third modified" form of his signature, which further established the date as 1660. The experts spoke with one voice: "Christ at Emmaus" was one of Vermeer's greatest masterpieces.

Van Meegeren's delight was mixed with bitterness. Certainly he now had reason for much satisfaction: formal recognition of the fact that he could paint as well as Vermeer. Nev-

ertheless, he bitterly reflected that this picture as a van Meegeren would be worth about $200. As a Vermeer he received
$250,000.

Of course there were compensations. Plainly he was on to a
good thing. Why should he not capitalize on his otherwise
unrecognized genius? If the art world was foolish enough to
pay vast sums for his pictures in the belief that they had been
painted by Vermeer three hundred years earlier, then he was

determined to profit by the ludicrous situation.

It was the war which brought him riches and also brought about his downfall. When Germany occupied Holland in 1940, the flourishing Dutch art business found that its services were in great demand by the conquerors. Top Nazis, Goering in particular, developed a sudden passion for art. Goering was busy accumulating his vast art collection at Berchtesgaden— later to be valued at a hundred million pounds.

Van Meegeren got busy once more, and between the years 1940 and 1945 produced no fewer than five masterpieces of Vermeer's little known middle period—"Christ and the Adulteress," "Head of Christ," the "Last Supper," "Isaac Blessing Jacob," and "Washing the Feet of Christ." He sold these for huge sums to private collectors and galleries, all of whom believed that he had discovered them. Goering acquired "Christ and the Adulteress" for $600,000.

By the end of the war van Meegeren was a millionaire. He owned a magnificent house in Amsterdam, as well as two night clubs, much property, and a notable art collection.

In 1945 a ruined Germany was overrun by Allied troops, and in May of that year a section of the Allied Fine Arts Commission examined Goering's fabulous collection at Berchtesgaden. Most of the pictures were easily recognizable as loot pilfered from all over Europe. One painting in particular puzzled the experts: the hitherto unknown Vermeer, "Christ and the Adulteress." While all the experts (deceived again by van Meegeren's remarkable gift for imitating Vermeer) were excited by this new find, the Dutch authorities were more interested in discovering who the dealer was who had traitorously sold this priceless Dutch possession to the Nazis. This was during the period of the great hunts for collaborators after the war. In Holland relentless investigations were launched tracking down those who had befriended the Nazis. The penalty for such treason could be death.

Inquiries finally led the police to the door of van Meegeren's splendid house in Amsterdam. Van Meegeren found himself facing charges of treason. When he claimed he had acquired the Vermeer from a noble Italian family forced to sell its possessions, he found he was suspected of being a collaborator who had passed on funds between Italy and Germany in the form of old masters. He also learned that he could be charged with the lesser offense of exporting works of art without permission, an act prohibited by Dutch law.

The police promptly took van Meegeren into custody, but when he refused to give the name of the Italian family from whom he claimed to have bought the Mermeer, he was locked up.

A night in jail brought him to a full realization of his position. He decided that the only way out of his dangerous predicament was to tell the truth. The following morning he confessed to the police that he had painted not only the Vermeer found in Goering's collection, but also a number of other so-called Vermeers; all of which the experts had certified as the master's and all of which had been sold for high prices.

This naturally caused a great sensation, though art critics ridiculed the idea they had been so completely hoodwinked. The man was mad. They had subjected these pictures to all the known tests—X-rays, quartz lamps, chemical analysis of the pigment. Besides, they said, there was no painter alive today who could have produced a major work like "Christ at Emmaus."

The Dutch authorities themselves were placed in something of a dilemma. Van Meegeren was released from prison while they decided what to do. If van Meegeren was speaking the truth then he had swindled not only Goering, which hardly mattered, but a number of other collectors out of large sums of money by selling them faked pictures. He had also made fools of some of Europe's most trusted and reliable art critics.

ON TRIAL Han van Meegeren, seated alone in box at left, listens to testimony during his trial at the Court of Amsterdam in 1947. Accused of defrauding art buyers of over $2,-000,000 by signing eight of his paintings with the names of Jan Vermeer and Pieter de Hoogh, van Meegeren was threatened with two years' imprisonment and with the destruction of the paintings in question. In the background are paintings by van Meegeren and Vermeer.

And that, to be sure, was a serious matter, however you looked at it. In Holland, which has produced some of the world's greatest painters, art is big business.

It was difficult to prosecute him. It was established that when he produced his so-called Vermeer discoveries, he had placed no price upon them and had left both the decision of their authenticity and their evaluation to the experts. How, therefore, could he be charged with selling them under false pretenses?

There was panic in the art world when a newly developed X-ray process revealed that some of the Vermeers which van Meegeren now claimed to have painted himself were in fact recently painted. Red-faced, embarrassed experts began to wonder whether van Meegeren was not telling the truth when he told them he had perpetrated the biggest art hoax in history.

There was one way in which the matter could be definitely settled. Would van Meegeren paint a copy of "Christ at Emmaus" under the eye of both the police and experts? Van Meegeren was not only willing, he was eager. More than that, he offered to paint an entirely new picture, the subject of which could be chosen by the art experts themselves.

This led to the creation of one of the most extraordinary pictures ever painted. It was titled "Christ in the Temple," and the men who watched van Meegeren paint it were confounded by his style, and by the remarkable skill with which he was able to reproduce the characteristics of Vermeer. An international panel of experts reviewed the entire case at the request of the Dutch Government and came to the conclusion that all the Vermeers in question were actually forgeries and that van Meegeren had painted them himself.

The public was delighted. Here was a man who had not only fooled the experts, but had proved that he could paint an old master as well as the old master himself. Van Meegeren

MASTER IMITATOR   Under the supervision of Dutch authorities, Han van Meegeren completes another "17th-century masterpiece" in 1945. The execution of this work, known as "Christ in the Temple" or "Christ amongst the Doctors," proved van Meegeren's mastery of both the Vermeer style and technique.

found himself hailed as a genius, and voted the second most popular man in Holland.

The authorities, however, were still in a quandary. They could not accuse van Meegeren of collaborating with the Germans. In fact it was possible to take some comfort in the thought that he had bilked Goering out of a large sum of money. But authorities being what they are, they could not let the matter rest. Van Meegeren had broken the rules. He must be made to pay.

There was only one crime he could now be charged with— that of forging Vermeer's signature. For that crime he was brought to trial in October, 1947. He pleaded guilty. A psychiatrist explained his actions in terms of a revenge complex.

Van Meegeren explained himself more explicitly to the judge. He loved painting Vermeers. He put all his talent and temperament into so doing. He went on painting them because it absorbed him as nothing else had ever absorbed him before.

"But as well as being absorbed, you were making a great deal of money out of it, weren't you?" asked the judge.

"Of course. I like money. As critics and dealers like money."

He said, with some exaggeration, that before he started to paint Vermeers he had been so hounded and persecuted by the critics that he was unable to sell his own paintings.

"But," said the court, "you were doing it for profit, weren't you?" It was as though profit were a shameful thing in itself; all artists should be starving in garrets.

"Does it matter what I say now?" asked van Meegeren.

It didn't. The verdict was against him. The court sentenced him to a year's imprisonment, finding him guilty, among other counts, of producing a picture which for eight years was accepted as an authentic masterpiece of the seventeenth century.

Sentencing him to prison proved unfortunate. Van Meegeren did not serve his sentence. Actually, he was never imprisoned. Within three months, broken and worn by his long ordeal, he was dead.

The fact that genuine van Meegerens are now fetching high prices may be ironical, but it is no surprise. It happens to most great artists after death.

INDEX